MOLECULAR
50 COURSE MEAL

AN AVANT-GARDE MENU INSPIRED BY MOLECULAR GASTRONOMY

Legal Deposit - Bibliothèque et Archives nationales du Québec, 2C
Legal Deposit - Library and Archives Canada, 2015

MOLECULE-R.COM

MOLECULAR RECIPES

TIPS & TRICKS

R-EVOLUTION D.I.Y. KITS

REFILLS & ACCESSORIES

MOLECULE-R.COM

#MolecularStyling

TABLE
OF CONTENTS

MOLECULAR TECHNIQUES   **10**

GELIFICATION   **14**

DEFINITION AND TECHNIQUE   15

TIPS & TRICKS   22

AGAR-AGAR   28

CARRAGEENAN   30

GELLAN GUM   32

GELATIN   34

SPHERIFICATION   **36**

DEFINITION AND TECHNIQUE   38

BASIC SPHERIFICATION   40

REVERSE SPHERIFICATION   40

FROZEN REVERSE SPHERIFICATION   40

TIPS & TRICKS   42

SODIUM ALGINATE   48

CALCIUM LACTATE   50

EMULSIFICATION   **52**

DEFINITION AND TECHNIQUE   54

TIPS & TRICKS   56

SOY LECITHIN   58

METHYLCELLULOSE   60

OTHER TRANSFORMATIONS   **62**

DEFINITION AND TECHNIQUE   64

SIPHON WHIPPING   64

SUSPENSION AND THICKENING   65

POWDERIZING   65

DEEP FREEZING   65

TIPS & TRICKS   66

XANTHAN GUM   68

MALTODEXTRIN   70

LIQUID NITROGEN   72

50 COURSE MEAL: RECIPES   74

1	CAVIAR & CHAMPAGNE	76
2	VOLATILE AMUSE-BOUCHE	78
3	DEEP-FROZEN GIN & TONIC	80
4	VODKA DICE & GAZPACHO	82
5	VOLATILE LAMB AMUSE-BOUCHE	84
6	NOUVEAU GENRE PANNA COTTA	86
7	DECONSTRUCTED MISO	88
8	DECONSTRUCTED CLAM RISOTTO	90
9	DECONSTRUCTED CASSEROLE	92
10	MODERN SPRING TARTARE	94
11	KALE CLOUD AND BEEF TARTARE	96
12	DECADENT DECONSTRUCTION	98
13	MODERNIZED TAGLIATELLE	100
14	HAM-WRAPPED MELON SUSHI	102
15	VEGETARIAN NIGIRI PLATTER	104
16	DECONSTRUCTED PLATTER	106
17	VIOLET SEA	108
18	JAPANESE SUNSET AIRS	110
19	GEOMETRIC TARTARE	112
20	VEAL STOCK CHIPS & MAPLE FILETS	114
21	QUINOA FORESTIERE WITH BERRY CAPSULES	116
22	ENCAPSULATED ENTREMETS	118
23	RARE RISOTTO	120
24	VEGETARIAN RISOTTO & PEARLS	122
25	NON-TRADITIONAL THANKSGIVING	124
26	SCALLOPS & POWDERIZED LIME	126
27	DECONSTRUCTED TACO	128
28	CAESAR BUBBLE	130
29	REINVENTED GREEK SALAD	132
30	AVANT-GARDE BEER TASTING	134
31	HONEY-GOLD ROSÉ JELLY	136
32	BERRY MONTAGE	138
33	MODERNIZED SAVOURY PARFAIT	140
34	DECONSTRUCTED COCOA	142
35	CHIA PUDDING WITH FRUIT CAVIAR	144
36	VOLATILE DESSERT ASPIC	146
37	MAPLE TRYPTICH	148
38	FRENCH NEW WAVE	150
39	ENCAPSULATED DAIQUIRI	152
40	HONEY CAVIAR & ROSE DICE	154
41	DECONSTRUCTED MOJITO	156
42	AVANT-GARDE CREME BRULEE	158
43	PUMPKIN PIE, REVISITED	160
44	MELON BALL	162
45	RED DECADENCE	164
46	MOUSSE QUINTET	166
47	TROPICAL CAPSULE DUO	168
48	JASMINE BALLOONS	170
49	CAPPUCCINO NOUVEAU GENRE	172
50	NEW OLD FASHIONED	174

MOLECULAR
50 COURSE MEAL

AN AVANT-GARDE MENU INSPIRED BY MOLECULAR GASTRONOMY

New technologies are now more integrated into the world of arts than ever before. Multimedia displays are set up in sculptures and exhibited in museums; the unexpected strength of new materials makes it possible to push the boundaries of architecture; and the public can now decide the ending of certain theatre plays using their smartphones.

The culinary arts are no exception to this trend and creative chefs are now inspired to incorporate cooking techniques and ingredients borrowed from the world of food science. For more than a decade, renowned, award-winning restaurants have been serving exotically flavored caviar, colorful, gravity-defying foams, bubbles that explode with flavors or even recreations of complex dishes in the form of simple spaghetti.

Obviously, the application of modern cooking techniques does not ensure a successful dish, but, as in all art forms, new technologies support the artistic process by allowing the artist to push creative boundaries. Like any artist, creative chefs provide their audience with an experience, and regardless of the technique, what matters most is the intensity of this experience.

Arising from the fusion of food science with culinary arts, molecular gastronomy is a gourmet trend whose artisans embrace innovation in order to create dishes that are truly multi-sensorial experiences. This cuisine is not at all opposed to the great culinary traditions; instead, it builds on past achievements and broadens the horizons by using resolutely modern techniques and ingredients. A new culinary era has arrived and is now accessible to amateur chefs!

MOLECULE-R PAVES THE WAY FOR A DEMOCRATIZATION OF MOLECULAR GASTRONOMY.

DEEP FREEZING

Cook with the cold
or create incomparably
smooth ice cream.

SPHERIFICATION

Encapsulate flavors
into bubbles that burst
in your mouth.

EMULSIFICATION

Create colorful foams
that intensify aromas.

MOLECULAR
GASTRONOMY TECHNIQUES

MOLECULAR GASTRONOMY CAN BE DEFINED AS THE FUSION OF FOOD SCIENCE AND CULINARY ARTS. NEW
TECHNOLOGIES AND NATURAL TEXTURING AGENTS CAN NOW BE USED TO DECONSTRUCT ANY DISHES
AND COCKTAILS, ENABLING ONE TO SERVE MOJITO BUBBLES AND MARTINI BITES, AS WELL AS BALSAMIC
VINEGAR PEARLS AND CHOCOLATE SPAGHETTIS. WITH MOLÉCULE-R PRODUCTS, A WORD OF CULINARY
POSSIBILITIES IS NOW WITHIN YOUR REACH!

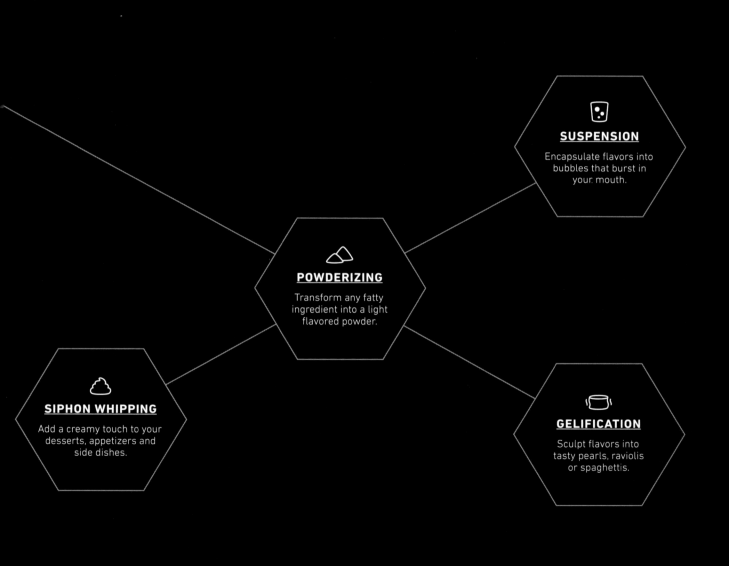

SUSPENSION

Encapsulate flavors into
bubbles that burst in
your mouth.

POWDERIZING

Transform any fatty
ingredient into a light
flavored powder.

SIPHON WHIPPING

Add a creamy touch to your
desserts, appetizers and
side dishes.

GELIFICATION

Sculpt flavors into
tasty pearls, raviolis
or spaghettis.

FOOD ADDITIVES

Research in food preservation is not a new development. Human beings have always sought to preserve foodstuffs first by chilling, drying or smoking meat, then by adding salt, vinegar and sugar. However, industrialization and the movement of populations to cities led to a completely different need: feeding thousands of people with fresh, processed, practical products that are stable during transportation and storage while retaining their organoleptic qualities. So-called "food additives" were gradually introduced to accommodate manufacturers throughout the food chain, but also to meet consumer demands for high-quality products.

Today, the term "food additive" covers nearly 2,500 chemicals that are added to foods for specific purposes such as preserving or processing and enhancing flavor or color. The use of additives in the food processing industry has become so widespread that they are now consumed on a daily basis by the general population.

This list includes coloring, stabilizers, acidifiers, preservatives, enzymes and texturing agents, but it is this last class of food additives that brings great pleasure to molecular gastronomy enthusiasts by creating culinary extravaganzas with unexpected surprises every time!

To share their passion for culinary creativity and experimentation, the young, dynamic team at MOLECULE-R Flavors has developed a complete line of texturing agents for amateur cooks to recreate some of the most spectacular techniques derived from molecular gastronomy. The cuisine of highly creative chefs is now accessible to everyone!

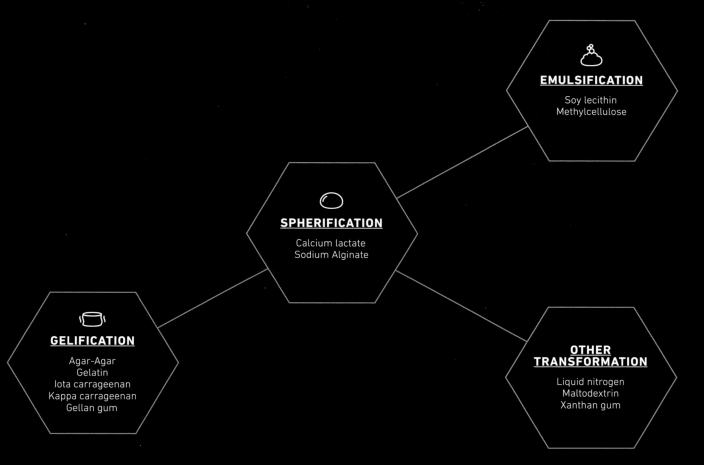

EMULSIFICATION

Soy lecithin
Methylcellulose

SPHERIFICATION

Calcium lactate
Sodium Alginate

GELIFICATION

Agar-Agar
Gelatin
Iota carrageenan
Kappa carrageenan
Gellan gum

OTHER TRANSFORMATION

Liquid nitrogen
Maltodextrin
Xanthan gum

Agar-Agar
Natural gelling agent extracted from red algae often used to create solid pearls, gel spaghettis and jellies.

Gelatin
Cold soluble gelatin that has the same textural properties and melt-in-the mouth effect as traditional gelatin.

Gellan Gum
Gelling agent obtained via fermentation and used to produce firm gels that slice cleanly & withstand high temperatures.

Iota Carrageenan
Natural gelling agent extracted from red algae and used to produce gels with a soft and elastic texture.

Kappa Carrageenan
Natural gelling agent extracted from red algae and used to produce gels with a firm and brittle texture.

Calcium Lactate
Calcium salt used with sodium alginate in the process of spherification.

Sodium Alginate
Natural gelling agent extracted from brown algae often combined with a calcium salt in the process of spherification

Methylcellulose
Natural emulsifier derived from cellulose, used to create denser foams and, when exposed to heat, to create gels that will melt as they cool down.

Soy Lecithin
Natural emulsifier extracted from soybeans, often used to shape watery solution into airs.

Liquid Nitrogen
A major component of air used in its liquid form to create the smoothest ice cream and cook with the cold.

Maltodextrin
Unsweet sugar mostly used in creative cooking as an aroma carrier, in the form of tasty powder that can be sprinkled over food preparations and dishes.

Xanthan Gum
Natural thickener derived from glucose via fermentation often used to stabilize emulsions and thicken sauces and drinks.

GELIFICATION
DEFINITION AND TECHNIQUE

SCULPT FLAVORS INTO TASTY PEARLS, RAVIOLIS OR SPAGHETTIS

GELIFICATION

SCULPT FLAVORS INTO TASTY PEARLS, RAVIOLIS OR SPAGHETTIS

The formation of a gel is one of the most common techniques in the industry. However, there is a tendency to disregard the great diversity of gels that can be made in cooking. Depending on the nature and concentrations of the gelling agent being used, the gel texture can range from supple and elastic to firm and brittle. This enables inventive cooks to experiment and attain the exact desired texture!

Despite the wide range of possible textures, the formation of a gel can simply be defined as a change from liquid to solid state. This process involves a rearrangement of the molecules that align and attach themselves until they form a network that traps the liquid. This network looks like meshes of a net that keep all of the particles in suspension, preventing their aggregation and the collapse of the structure.

Several well-known molecules are able to form gels. The most traditional are found everywhere: flours, tapioca or corn starch, eggs and gelatin. However, non-traditional gelling agents are becoming more commonplace in the market and are widely used in molecular gastronomy: hydrocolloids

HYDROCOLLOIDS

The use of hydrocolloids in cooking makes it possible to form gels with various textures at temperatures, pH levels and with foods that are impossible to gel with common gelling agents. In addition, the concentration needed to achieve the desired result is often lower, which is a significant advantage that avoids excessive changes in flavor. So it is not surprising to find these texturizing agents in a whole range of consumer products.

The definition of hydrocolloid is not quite established, but the origin of the word greatly helps to understand the meaning. Hydrocolloids become hydrated in water (hence the prefix "hydro"). Once the colloidal solution has formed, it hinders the mobility of water until it becomes thickened or gelled. The long molecules that join together to form a gel through various preparation stages are called polymers. The strength and type of connections determine the characteristics of the gel.

IMPLEMENTATION

As with all culinary techniques, to successfully make a gel using hydrocolloids requires precision and compliance with certain key steps. Considering how easy it is to make instant puddings, this seems a bit excessive, but to guarantee success, there is no room for carelessness!

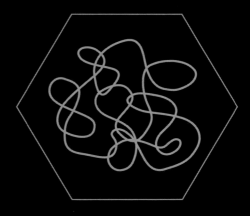

DISPERSION

Initially, the hydrocolloid particles dispersed in water detach from each other, thus allowing liquid to penetrate into and swell the molecule, and then dissolve.

DISPERSION is an essential step for the formation of a gel and for the thickening of a preparation. An improperly dispersed gelling agent will stick together and form lumps that will alter the subsequent formation of the gel. Dispersion must allow the gelling agent molecules to be completely surrounded by water by separating the powder particles. For several hydrocolloids (agar-agar, carrageenan, sodium alginate, gellan gum), this requires vigorous stirring of the mixture with cold water.

HYDRATION then allows water to penetrate inside the hydrocolloid molecules, which then facilitate reactions, as it is surrounded by water and suspended in the solvent. This step can be done by gradually heating or chilling the liquid. Agar-agar, carrageenans, some gelatins and gellan gum require heating to hydrate. Alginate hydration requires cooling; the process is described in detail in the section on spherification.

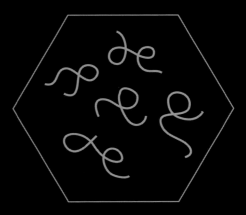

HYDRATION

Molecules dispersed in the solution are essentially linear polymer chains with few similarities among them at this stage. Once hydrated, the long molecules no longer have any defined structure and are rather randomly organized in the solution.

FORMATION of most hydrocolloids occurs after hot hydration, when the temperature drops to a gelling temperature that is specific to each additive. Although some gels are formed before reaching room temperature, others require refrigeration.

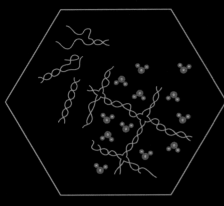

FORMATION

As the solution cools, the polymer chains twist together and form double helices with other molecules while bonding one molecule to another.

OTHER CHARACTERISTICS

The gel's final texture varies greatly from one hydrocolloid to another, but several other properties specific to each of the additives can also influence the selection in the development of a recipe.

The strength of bonds between polymer chains influences the gel's texture in the mouth. However, it should also be noted that some hydrocolloids form gels in the presence of ions, such as calcium, magnesium, or potassium. Carrageenans and gellan gum are good examples, making these additives a preferred choice in dairy-based products. Sodium alginate, on the other hand, only reacts in the presence of calcium ions. For more details, read the section on spherification.

The melting point of gels is another characteristic that can be exploited in cooking. A gel obtained from gelatin will melt at a temperature of 99°F (37°C), the same temperature as the human body. Gelatin-based jellies thus create a melt-in-the-mouth sensation. In contrast, agar-agar-based gels have a melting point around 194°F (90°C), which gives these dishes the significant advantage of being able to be served hot.

It should also be mentioned that some hydrocolloids simply have no melting point. The resulting gels are called thermoirreversible, that is, once the bonds between the polymer chains have formed, they cannot be broken. For example, gellan gum-based gels will never melt at temperatures used in cooking and may therefore

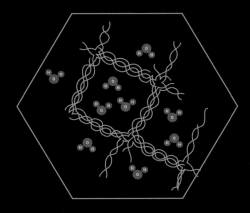

STRONG BONDS

A strong bond between the molecules is created when multiple links are formed between the double helices. The resulting gel will be firmer and more brittle.

even be incorporated into stewed dishes!

The gel solution's acidity can also affect the result and therefore some gels do not congeal in the presence of highly acidic ingredients. It is also important to note that the degree of transparency of gels will vary based on the gelling agent chosen. Agar-agar will usually produce cloudy gels, whereas kappa carrageenan and gellan gum will produce gels whose transparency ranges from slightly opaque to opaque. Finally, sodium alginate, gelatin and iota carrageenan produce completely clear gels.

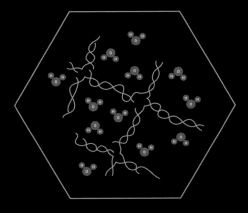

WEAK BONDS

A weak bond between the molecules will result in softer, more elastic gels.

	AGAR-AGAR	SODIUM ALGINATE	IOTA CARRAGEENAN
Origin	Red algae	Brown algae	Red algae
Clarity	Semi-opaque	Transparent, clear	Semi-opaque
Mouthfeel	Gritty when highly concentrated, soft when lowly concentrated	Soft	Creamy
Texture	Thermoreversible, firm, brittle gel	Thermoirreversible, flexible gel in the presence of calcium, thickener in the absence of calcium	Thermoreversible, flexible gel in the presence of calcium, soft gel in the absence of calcium
Dispersion	In cold or hot water, using a spoon or whisk	In cold water, using a handblender; can be improved by mixing with any powdery ingredient	In cold water, using a handblender; can be improved by mixing with sugar or alcohol
Hydration (activation)	T > 194°F	In cold or hot water	T > 158°F
Setting	Quick (a few minutes); T < 95-113°F	Quick (a few minutes); independently of temperature	Medium (15 minutes); T < 104-158°F
Melting	176-194°F	Does not melt; prolonged heating may destabilize the gel	113-176°F
Prohibitor	Requires prolonged heating with highly acidic or highly basic solutions	Acidic ingredients (pH < 4) and very salty solutions	n/a
Promoter	Sugar	Calcium (essential for gelling)	Calcium
Freezer stable	No	Yes	Yes

KAPPA CARRAGEENAN	COLD SOLUBLE GELATIN	GELLAN GUM (low acyl)
Red algae	Animal protein	Bacterial fermentation
Transparent, clear	Transparent, clear	Transparent
Firm when highly concentrated, soft when lowly concentrated	Soft, melts in the mouth	Firm and brittle
Thermoreversible, brittle gel in the presence of potassium, firm gel in the absence of potassium	Thermoreversible, soft, elastic gel	Thermoirreversible, hard, brittle gel
In cold water, using a handblender; can be improved by mixing with sugar or alcohol	In cold water, using a handblender; can be improved by mixing with any powdery ingredient	In cold water, using a spoon or whisk; can be improved by mixing with sugar or alcohol
T > 158°F	T > 68°F	T > 203°F
Medium (15 minutes); T < 86-140°F	Long (a few hours); T < 59°F	Quick (a few minutes); T < 50-140°F
104-176°F	77-104°F	Does not melt
Salts	Salts, acidic ingredients, solutions with a high alcohol concentration, prolonged heating, kiwi, pineapple, peach, mango	Highly acidic solutions as well as solutions with a high calcium or sodium concentration will prevent hydration
Potassium	Milk, sugar, solutions with a low alcohol concentration	Highly acidic solutions as well as solutions with a high calcium or sodium concentration will promote gelling
No	No	Yes

AGAR-AGAR PEARLS

AGAR-AGAR CAN BE USED TO SCULPT PRACTICALLY ANY SOLUTION INTO A GEL, BE IT IN THE SHAPE OF A PEARL, A SPAGHETTI OR A SHEET.

PRINCIPLE

Agar-agar's gelifying properties are activated when the solution is heated to a temperature of 194°F. The gelification process itself is then triggered when the solution cools down to temperatures ranging between 90°F and 110°F. The gel produced will be reversible, so it can be re-melted and re-shaped.

To create pearls, the solution containing agar-agar should be brought to a boil first and then dripped into a cold oil to trigger gelification. So long as the pearls can cool down before they sink to the bottom of the container of oil, they will be perfectly round.

PREPARATION STEPS

01 Place a tall glass of vegetable oil in the freezer, allowing it to cool for at least 30 minutes.

N.B. THE OIL SHOULD BE COLD ENOUGH AND THE GLASS TALL ENOUGH FOR THE GELIFICATION PROCESS TO BE COMPLETED BEFORE THE DROPS OF THE AGAR-AGAR SOLUTION REACH THE BOTTOM OF THE GLASS.

02 Heat the preparation and sprinkle in one sachet (2g) of agar-agar.

N.B. STIR PREPARATION UNTIL THE AGAR-AGAR IS COMPLETELY DISSOLVED.

03 Bring the preparation to a boil in order to activate the agar-agar's properties.

N.B. REMOVE FROM STOVE AS SOON AS IT STARTS BOILING; THE PREPARATION SHOULD REACH A TEMPERATURE OF APPROXIMATELY 194°F. EXCESS BOILING COULD ALTER THE TASTE OF CERTAIN INGREDIENTS.

04 Using a pipette, drip droplets of the agar-agar preparation into the cold oil.

N.B. THE OIL SHOULDN'T BE TOO COLD OR NEAR-FROZEN, AS THIS WILL MAKE THE DROPLETS FLOAT. SHOULD THIS HAPPEN, KEEP DRIPPING DROPLETS OF THE HOT PREPARATION INTO THE OIL; THE DROPLETS WILL START SINKING AS THE OIL WARMS UP.

05 Collect the pearls using a slotted spoon or a sieve and rinse the pearls with water.

THE SOLUTION TO BE TRANSFORMED

Prepare approximately ¾ cup of a solution to be transformed into pearls. The acidity of the ingredients used will not impact the gelification process. However, the addition of sugar will strengthen the gel.

Warning : Denser, thicker solutions such as honey-based or syrup-based solutions can be diluted in order to ensure that they contain enough water to hydrate the agar-agar.

SERVING AND PRESERVATION

Store the pearls in a closed container in the fridge for several days if needed. The pearls can also be left to macerate in the oil used in previous steps if the taste of the oil fits with that of the pearls.

Rinsing the pearls with water is optional if the taste of the oil used in previous steps fits with that of the pearls. The same oil could also be used to extend the pearls' fridgelife.

To serve hot, warm up the pearls by submerging them in hot water.

PLEASE NOTE

Shapeless or flat pearls indicate that the oil was not cold enough at the time of dripping the preparation, or that the glass used wasn't deep enought.

AGAR-AGAR SPAGHETTI

AGAR-AGAR CAN BE USED TO SCULPT PRACTICALLY ANY SOLUTION INTO A GEL, BE IT IN THE SHAPE OF A PEARL, A SPAGHETTI OR A SHEET.

PRINCIPLE

Agar-agar's gelifying properties are activated when the solution is heated to a temperature of 194°F. The gelification process itself is then triggered when the solution cools down to temperatures ranging between 90°F and 110°F. The gel produced will be reversible, so it can be re-melted and re-shaped.

To create spaghetti, the solution containing agar-agar should be brought to a boil, then injected into a silicone tube, then allowed to cool down before being removed.

PREPARATION STEPS

01 Fill a tall container with cold water and ice cubes.

    N.B.   VERY COLD WATER WILL ACCELERATE THE COOLING DOWN OF THE AGAR-AGAR PREPARATION AS WELL AS THE GELIFICATION PROCESS.

02 Heat the preparation and sprinkle in one sachet (2g) of agar-agar.

    N.B.   STIR PREPARATION UNTIL THE AGAR-AGAR IS COMPLETELY DISSOLVED.

03 Bring the preparation to a boil in order to activate the agar-agar's properties.

    N.B.   REMOVE FROM STOVE AS SOON AS IT STARTS BOILING; THE PREPARATION SHOULD REACH A TEMPERATURE OF APPROXIMATELY 194°F. EXCESS BOILING COULD ALTER THE TASTE OF CERTAIN INGREDIENTS.

04 Fill a food syringe with the preparation and affix a silicone tube to the syringe.

    N.B.   POUR THE HOT AGAR-AGAR PREPARATION INTO A CONTAINER THAT WILL FACILITATE FURTHER MANIPULATIONS.

05 Using the syringe, fill the silicone tube with the preparation, which should still be hot.

    N.B.   SMALL SOLID PARTICLES REMAINING IN A POORLY FILTERED PREPARATION COULD BLOCK THE TIP OF THE SYRINGE.

06 Submerge the tube into the iced water and let cool down for 3 minutes.

    N.B.   TO BE COMPLETED, THE GELIFICATION PROCESS REQUIRES THAT THE AGAR-AGAR PREPARATION COOLS DOWN COMPLETELY WHILE IN THE TUBE; OTHERWISE, THE SPAGHETTI WILL NOT HOLD ITS SHAPE ONCE IT IS REMOVED FROM THE TUBE.

07 Using a food syringe, inject air into the tube to extract the spaghetti while gradually increasing the pressure applied on the syringe's piston.

THE SOLUTION TO BE TRANSFORMED

Prepare approximately ¾ cup of a solution to be transformed into a spaghetti, and filter if needed. The acidity of the ingredients used will not impact the gelification process. However, the addition of sugar will strengthen the gel.

Denser, thicker solutions such as honey-based or syrup-based solutions can be diluted in order to ensure that they contain enough water to hydrate the agar-agar.

Warning : Small solid particles remaining in a poorly filtered preparation could block the tip of the syringe.

SERVING AND PRESERVATION

Store the spaghetti in a closed container in the fridge for several days if needed.

To serve hot, warm up the the spaghetti by submerging them in hot water.

PLEASE NOTE

A spaghetti formed using too little agar-agar will be fragile and will not hold its shape. Should this happen, re-heat the gelified preparation while incorporating more agar-agar, and repeat the previous steps.

A spaghetti formed using too much agar-agar will lack elasticity and will tend to break easily. Should this happen, re-heat the gelified preparation while diluting it, and repeat the previous steps.

AGAR-AGAR CANNELLONI

AGAR-AGAR CAN BE USED TO SCULPT PRACTICALLY ANY SOLUTION INTO A GEL, BE IT IN THE SHAPE OF A PEARL, A SPAGHETTI OR A SHEET.

PRINCIPLE

Agar-agar's gelifying properties are activated when the solution is heated to a temperature of 194°F. The gelification process itself is then triggered when the solution cools down to temperatures ranging between 90°F and 110°F. The gel produced will be reversible, so it can be re-melted and re-shaped.

To create cannelloni, the solution containing agar-agar should be brought to a boil, then evenly spread on a smooth surface and allowed to cool down and congeal. The thin sheet of gel thus formed can be rolled up and even stuffed.

PREPARATION STEPS

01 Heat the preparation and sprinkle in one sachet (2g) of agar-agar.

N.B.   STIR PREPARATION UNTIL THE AGAR-AGAR IS COMPLETELY DISSOLVED.

02 Bring the preparation to a boil in order to activate the agar-agar's properties.

N.B.   REMOVE FROM STOVE AS SOON AS IT STARTS BOILING; THE PREPARATION SHOULD REACH A TEMPERATURE OF APPROXIMATELY 194°F. EXCESS BOILING COULD ALTER THE TASTE OF CERTAIN INGREDIENTS.

03 Pour the preparation onto a plate or a baking sheet and tilt IT so that the preparation spreads thinly (1/8 inch thick) and evenly.

04 Let cool for at least 5 minutes.

N.B.   TO BE COMPLETED. THE GELIFICATION PROCESS REQUIRES THAT THE AGAR-AGAR PREPARATION COOLS DOWN COMPLETELY; OTHERWISE, THE CANNELLONI WILL NOT HOLD ITS SHAPE DURING MANIPULATION.

05 Using a knife, Cut the gel into rectangular pieces.

N.B.   STIR PREPARATION UNTIL THE AGAR-AGAR IS COMPLETELY DISSOLVED.

06 Deposit a small amount of hot or cold filling onto the sheet of gel to create a cannelloni.

N.B.   DO NOT PUT TOO MUCH FILLING TO EASILY FOLD THE CANNELLONI. BRING THE PREPARATION TO A BOIL IN ORDER TO ACTIVATE THE AGAR-AGAR'S PROPERTIES.

THE SOLUTION TO BE TRANSFORMED

Prepare approximately ¾ cup of a solution to be transformed into a cannelloni. The acidity of the ingredients used will not impact the gelification process. However, the addition of sugar will strengthen the gel.

Warning : Denser, thicker solutions such as honey-based or syrup-based solutions can be diluted in order to ensure that they contain enough water to hydrate the agar-agar.

SERVING AND PRESERVATION

Store gel sheets in a closed container in the fridge for several days if needed.

To serve hot, warm up gel sheets by submerging them in hot water. Then place warm filling onto the warm gel sheet and create the cannelloni.

PLEASE NOTE

An overly thick gel sheet or a gel sheet that was formed using too much agar-agar will tend to break when folded. Should this happen, re-heat the gelified preparation while diluting it, and repeat the previous steps.

An overly thin gel sheet or a gel sheet that was formed using too little agar-agar will not hold its shape when manipulated. Should this happen, re-heat the gelified preparation while incorporating more agar-agar, and repeat the previous steps.

AGAR-AGAR

NATURAL GELLING AGENT EXTRACTED FROM RED ALGAE OFTEN USED TO CREATE SOLID PEARLS, GEL SPAGHETTIS AND JELLIES.

Although its exotic name may puzzle some consumers, agar-agar has long been known in Japan where consumption and use of algae for culinary purposes goes back centuries. The gelling substance was discovered by accident in 1658. A cook at an inn discarded some left-over gelidium seaweed soup served at dinner. It froze, thawed and dried during adverse weather before finally being found by its creator. He then boiled and cooled the residue and discovered that the resulting jelly had enhanced culinary properties.

It is still possible to find hand-made agar-agar. Although the current manufacturing process still uses the same basic steps (boiling, freezing, thawing, drying), it has however been adapted to modern industrial methods, which obtain a more stable and safer product through effective extraction methods. But the raw material remains the same as when agar-agar was first discovered: Rhodophyceae, red algae, including several genera other than gelidium are now harvested (gracilaria, pterocladia, gellidiella).

In the industry, algae are first washed and then treated with an acid or an alkali to facilitate extraction or to increase the final product's gelling capacity. The plants are then boiled under pressure, filtered and cooled. Next, two methods are used to extract water from the product: either a freezing and thawing process or mechanical pressure is applied to the gel formed upon boiling. Finally, the plant gum obtained is dried and then ground according to the desired form: powder, flakes, bars or threads.

The advantage of this polysaccharide for the food industry and cooking lies in its ability to form a reversible gel which, unlike a gelatin-based gel, requires a low concentration and allows greater flexibility in the temperature at which it can be used. In fact, agar-agar gel only melts at a temperature of around 194°F (90°C) and congeals faster once boiled, as soon as its temperature drops to about 104°F (40°C). When mixed with cold water, agar-agar is insoluble. When it is boiled in water, its polysaccharide linear structure curls and forms helices that then join a more complex arrangement, trapping the water upon cooling.

The result is a brittle, cloudy gel, which allows cooks to sculpt delicious liquid mixtures in many unusual forms such as spaghetti, beads, or thin, tasty sheets that can be rolled.Agar-agar also offers the advantage of not requiring the addition of molecules or other ingredients besides water, since agar-agar molecules bind together due to the hydrogen ions already present in water. In addition, this hydrocolloid can be used with various sugars, proteins and more acidic foods such as fruit. It is worth noting that the addition of large amounts of sugar, up to 60% of the solution, will further strengthen the gel. The use of agar-agar is definitely flexible, but you have to be careful: tannic acid found in squash, apples or plums may hinder the formation of the gel if they are used in large quantities in the gel preparation.

DID YOU KNOW?

01

AGAR-AGAR effectively replaces animal gelatin in a vegetarian diet and has virtually no taste or color.

02

AGAR-AGAR is used in microbiology as a culture medium for bacteria, cells, yeasts and molds.

03

AGAR-AGAR is included in some slimming diets due to its high-fiber, low calorie satiating effect.

04

AGAR-AGAR is used as a stabilizer, emulsifier, and gelling and thickening agent in the food processing industry, which accounts for 90% of its total production.

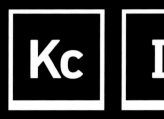

CARRAGEENANS

NATURAL GELLING AGENT DERIVED FROM RED ALGAE, USED TO CREATE SMOOTH, ELASTIC GELS (IOTA CARRAGEENAN) OR FIRM, BRITTLE GELS (KAPPA CARRAGEENAN).

Used for a long time in Ireland, where it is also known as carrageen moss, the inhabitants of this country gave carrageenan its name. As it creates a creamy texture, this dried seaweed was originally boiled with milk to make pudding or thicken infant formula.

Like agar-agar, carrageenan is a hydrocolloid obtained from the cell walls of red algae. As there is a large variety of algae used for extracting the product, their chemical characteristics differ greatly and allow a multitude of uses depending on their origins and composition. Three types of carrageenan stand out depending on the predominance of sugar in their structure: kappa, iota and lambda, which come respectively from Kappachycus alvarezii, Eucheuma denticulatum and Chondrus crispus. Other seaweed is also harvested, including Furcellaria, Gigartina and Iridaea.

The main goal of processing is to isolate the hydrocolloid locked inside the algae. To do this, chemical agents (salts, alcohols, alkalies) and mechanical means, such as filtration, concentration, drying and grinding, are applied to the plant. The salts chosen to extract carrageenan greatly depend on the desired final product and desired gelling properties, since they cause molecular rearrangement. Production of carrageenan requires great precision, in-depth knowledge of its gelling and thickening properties, and standardized procedures in order to create identical mixtures every time and thereby ensure production consistency.

Due to its composition, kappa carrageenan forms a brittle, firm gel, which is potentiated and stabilized by the presence of potassium. Many layers of kappa molecules join together forming double helices that produce this particular texture. The final product is greatly affected by salts, sugar or proteins, such as those present in milk. Interactions between positive and negative charges of the additive and solution create a network similar to the meshes of a net, which keep all of the particles in suspension, preventing their aggregation and the collapse of the structure.

Iota carrageenan has greater affinity with calcium, although it is not necessary in order for it to congeal. Calcium, like potassium with kappa carrageenan, lodges between double helices to stabilize the gel. Iota carrageenan usually produces an elastic gel that does not degrade if it is frozen and thawed. It also forms a stronger gel in the presence of starch.

The third type of carrageenan, lambda, significantly differs from the other two. It does not gel, with or without the addition of ions, but is used to thicken dairy products. It is used less often, but is sometimes combined with kappa to change the texture of certain products.

Finally, it is important to note that acidic foods destroy polysaccharide chains and prevent the product from congealing. It is therefore essential to add this type of ingredient at the very last moment.

DID YOU KNOW?

01

CARRAGEENANS ensure the consistency of various dairy products such as cottage cheese and ice cream, as they prevent the separation of proteins.

02

CARRAGEENANS keep cocoa particles in suspension in chocolate milk.

03

CARRAGEENANS improve the texture of processed products such as sauces, dairy desserts and salad dressings, as they increase the products' viscosity.

04

CARRAGEENANS trap moisture in cured meats to give them a juicy texture.

GELLAN GUM

GELLING AGENT OBTAINED VIA FERMENTATION USED TO PRODUCE FIRM GELS THAT SLICE CLEANLY AND WITHSTAND HIGH TEMPERATURES.

Gellan gum is a polysaccharide whose origin differs from that of other hydrocolloids presented so far. Its rather recent discovery was the result of industrial research on gum from bacterial fermentation. Sphingomonas elodea bacteria transform simple sugars, phosphate, nitrogen and nutrients into chains of more complex sugars. Once the process has been completed, the microorganisms are eliminated by pasteurization.

Precipitation in alcohol and acyl group clarification or elimination processes are applied to the gum to further transform it. Four derivatives are manufactured in the industry, each with different properties. Two forms are more widely used in cooking: high-acyl and low-acyl gellan gum.

HIGH-ACYL GELLAN GUM

High-acyl gellan gum produces a supple, elastic texture, which is the result of the well-known acyl groups, allowing the formation of helices that trap water. Upon hydration, the gum is insensitive to the presence of calcium or sodium ions, which do not significantly affect the formation of a gel. However, heat is necessary to properly hydrate the molecule, whereas the presence of sugars or acids in excessive quantity can interfere with this crucial step. The gel melts and re-sets at about 158°F to 176°F (70°C to 80°C).

LOW-ACYL GELLAN GUM

Low-acyl gellan gum is more commonly used in molecular gastronomy to make firm, brittle gels that tolerate temperatures up to 284°F (140°C). For this reason, it is preferred in the preparation of hot dishes. However, it must be handled with great care, as it is significantly more sensitive to the presence of ions than its high-acyl counterpart. Hard water, as well as the presence of sugar or an acid solution medium, slows down the hydration process, which requires a higher temperature.

The best way to properly hydrate this product is to mix it with demineralized water or milk, or use sequestering agents and mix vigorously. The sequestering agents used are salts (sodium citrate, sodium hexametaphosphate) which, when dissolved in water, attach to the ions, making them unavailable for the gum in the solution and thus allowing it to hydrate at a lower temperature. The gel forms upon cooling due to the ions present in the food added to the mixture, or by the addition of other ions such as calcium, sodium, magnesium or potassium salts. There are a great variety of solutions with which low-acyl gellan gum can form gels, which greatly increases its possible uses.

DID YOU KNOW?

01

GELLAN GUM replaces agar-agar in culture media that must be maintained at very high temperatures.

02

GELLAN GUM is used in gelatinous beverages that are popular in Asia, but marketing abroad proved to be difficult, particularly in North America with the beverage "Orbitz."

03

GELLAN GUM adheres salt crystals that are sprayed onto pretzels, without adding fat.

04

GELLAN GUM often replaces pectin in sugar-free jams and is added to dry cake mixes to maintain enough moisture during cooking.

GELATIN

COLD SOLUBLE GELATIN THAT HAS THE SAME TEXTURAL PROPERTIES AND MELT-IN-THE MOUTH EFFECT AS TRADITIONAL GELATIN.

Gelatin is probably one of the best known additives outside the food industry. Its discovery dates back to the Egyptians, who used it to make glue. Since then, its use has obviously become greatly diversified!

Gelatin is naturally formed when meat, bones or skin are slowly boiled to make a stock or stew. Once cooled, the mixture forms a jelly. Gelatin was known and used in cooking well before the product was marketed at the end of the 19th century, when an American named Charles Knox introduced it on the U.S. market in the form of a powder.

Unlike other additives presented in this book, gelatin is of animal origin. Its structure is therefore a blend of amino acids, the components of proteins. Gelatin is derived from collagen found in the skin and bones of beef, pork, fish or poultry. Once these parts are ground, an acid or alkaline treatment is applied to them for days, or even months, after which they are boiled and cleared of impurities through filtration. A concentration of the solution and a high temperature treatment are applied before cooling and drying. On the market, gelatin comes in powder form, flakes, sheets or granules. The origin of the raw material and the processing obviously affect the gel's final strength.

During cooling, chains of amino acids form helices that trap water in a structure resembling a fishing net. Due to gelatin's properties, it can be added to food as a gelling agent, stabilizer, emulsifier and crystal inhibitor. The gel formed is thermoreversible and melts at about body temperature, which creates a melt-in-the-mouth sensation.

The main criticism of gelatin concerns its animal origin and the fear that it may contain contaminants or unwanted bacteria. However, gelatin purity regulations are very strict and only animals that are tested and approved for human consumption are used in the product. In the industry, gelatin is considered an ingredient rather than an additive and no consumption limits have been set.

DID YOU KNOW?

01

GELATIN lends its name to the colored film used on light projectors, as colored gelatin-based gels originally served the same purpose in the first lighting equipment.

02

GELATIN is one of the main components in gel capsules that protect drugs and affect their absorption rate.

03

GELATIN is found in some cosmetics, as one of its derivatives, "hydrolyzed collagen," is known for its anti-aging effects.

04

GELATIN is used to hold silver halide crystals in an emulsion in photographic films.

SPHERIFICATION
DEFINITION AND TECHNIQUE

ENCAPSULATE FLAVORS INTO BUBBLES THAT BURST IN YOUR MOUTH

SPHERIFICATION

ENCAPSULATE FLAVORS INTO BUBBLES THAT BURST IN YOUR MOUTH.

So-called spherification is based on a food re-engineering manufacturing process. For years, the food industry has been using this process to re-engineer fruit, vegetable or meat purees into pieces whose form and texture are very similar to the basic ingredient. For example, what appears to be a piece of bell pepper stuffed into pitted olives is actually a gelled and remolded puree. By doing so, the industry is able to maintain consistent uniformity in the appearance of products. In addition, by using puree rather than whole foods, the industry can achieve substantial cost savings.

One thing is for certain: when Catalan chef Ferran Adrià of the famous restaurant El Bulli in Spain adopted and perfected this technique, he had something else in mind other than recycling raw material! In molecular gastronomy, spherification is now defined as the encapsulation of a liquid inside different sized spheres that burst in the mouth.

The wall trapping the liquid inside the sphere consists of a gel formed by a process similar in some respects to the one described in the preceding section on gelling. The additive used is sodium alginate, and just like in the gelling process using carrageenans or gellan gum, the presence of ions is essential for the formation of the gel. In the case of a sodium alginate gel, the presence of calcium ions is required so that the long alginate molecules can align and bind to finally form a gel. To better understand the ability of sodium alginate to form a gel, let's take a closer look at the molecule.

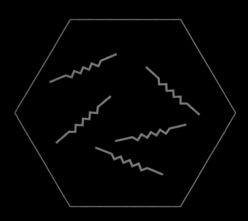

SODIUM ALGINATE MOLECULE

Sodium alginate is made up of long molecules
that look like zigzags.

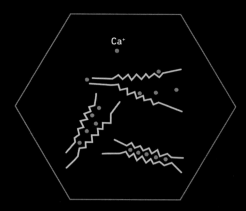

CALCIUM IONS REACTION

The long molecule threads are attracted to each other by calcium ions and create a structure that resembles a box of eggs.

Alginate reacts with any calcium that naturally occurs or that has been added to the ingredient to be spherified. For example, we could make a pudding by simply adding sodium alginate to a preparation of milk and sugar, as milk is naturally rich in calcium. Applying this principle, we can precisely control the moment when the calcium and alginate come into contact and thereby diversify the liquids to be gelled and the forms obtained.

Depending on the source of calcium ions, two types of spherification can be used:

〈 01 〉 BASIC SPHERIFICATION

〈 02 〉 REVERSE SPHERIFICATION

Both techniques can be used to create different sized spheres. However, basic spherification is preferred to create small balls, or caviar, whereas reverse spherification is the preferred method to form larger spheres, also called flavor bubbles.

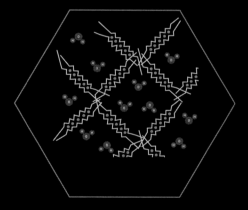

GEL FORMATION

This process involves a rearrangement of the molecules that align and attach themselves until they form a network that traps the liquid. This network looks like meshes of a net that keep all of the particles in suspension, preventing their aggregation and the collapse of the structure.

BASIC SPHERIFICATION

Basic spherification consists in immersing a liquid containing sodium alginate in a high-calcium bath. Calcium ions then migrate from the sphere's exterior to its interior.

As a large amount of calcium ions remains present in the caviar's wall, even a water rinse will not completely slow down the gelling of the wall, which will thicken until the sphere's interior is completely gelled. Since an in-the-mouth flavor burst is usually desired, it is recommended to serve the caviar as quickly as possible after its formation.

It is important to note that the addition of the sodium alginate solution to the preparation to be transformed significantly dilutes it. So, for maximum flavor, be sure to transform solutions that are highly flavorful; otherwise the taste will be rather bland. Sodium alginate will also thicken the preparation. Since the preparation is thicker and less intense in flavor, basic spherification is not recommended for creating large flavor bubbles. However, it is the most practical technique to create small beads, commonly known as flavor caviar.

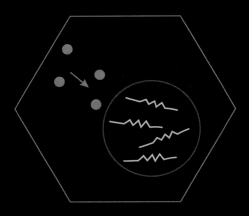

BASIC SPHERIFICATION

A solution containing sodium alginate is poured into a high-calcium bath. Calcium ions migrate towards the solution to be spherified and then trigger the membrane's gelification.

REVERSE SPHERIFICATION

As its name suggests, compared with basic spherification, reverse spherification involves a permutation in the process of immersing sodium alginate and calcium salt. The principle is to pour a high-calcium solution in a bath in which sodium alginate has been dissolved. Calcium ions then migrate from the sphere's interior to its wall.

Unlike what happens in basic spherification, it is possible to slow down the wall's thickening process, since rinsing removes excess sodium alginate on the sphere's contours. In the absence of alginate molecules, calcium ions have no effect and the sphere's interior remains liquid. Once rinsed, flavor bubbles can be stored and served sometime after their formation.

Dissolving sodium alginate in a solution significantly thickens it. The sodium alginate bath is therefore very thick and some solutions that are too watery simply cannot penetrate it: the result will look more like a deformed lump of gel than a sphere!

When choosing preparations to be spherified, it is best to work with liquid bases that are naturally thick and high in calcium such as cream, yogurt and certain purees. It is also possible to thicken the preparation to be transformed using a thickening agent such as xanthan gum to minimize the density gap with the sodium alginate bath. However, to spherify very watery solutions, frozen reverse spherification is recommended.

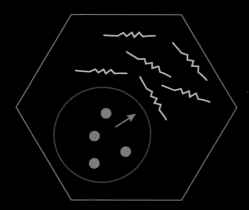

REVERSE SPHERIFICATION

A solution containing calcium is immersed in a high-sodium alginate bath. Calcium ions migrate from the sphere's interior to its exterior, thus forming a gel wall.

FROZEN REVERSE SPHERIFICATION

Freezing solutions enables greater precision in the final form and overcomes many of the limitations and constraints of spherification. The technique is straightforward and very similar to reverse spherification.

A pinch of calcium salt is first added to the preparation to be transformed, after which the preparation is molded and frozen. The ice cubes thus produced are then immersed in a sodium alginate bath and rinsed. You no longer have to worry about the preparation's texture, since the ice cubes easily penetrate the surface of the sodium alginate bath. So you can transform completely liquid solutions for an even more spectacular in-the-mouth effect!

OTHER CHARACTERISTICS

Sodium alginate-based gels are irreversible and therefore can be served hot. To do this, simply immerse the spheres in hot water and wait until the heat is absorbed. In addition, they are resistant to freezing and thawing. The fact that they can congeal cold without prior heating is also a certain advantage.

Nevertheless, it is important to note that the spherification process may be hindered by a high level of acidity or alcohol. Frozen reverse spherification avoids most of these contraindications, obviously provided that the preparation can be frozen.

Finally, be wary of unknown calcium sources that could congeal the preparation without warning. If the tap water is particularly high in calcium, it would be preferable to use bottled water. Also, do not pour the alginate bath down a narrow pipe; otherwise, it could form a blockage!

BASIC SPHERIFICATION

BASIC SPHERIFICATION IS IDEAL TO CREATE CAVIAR THAT WILL LIBERATE THEIR FLAVORS WHILE BURSTING IN YOUR MOUTH! FOR LARGER SPHERES, IT IS RECOMMENDED TO USE REVERSE SPHERIFICATION OR REVERSE FROZEN SPHERIFICATION.

PRINCIPLE

When a solution containing sodium alginate is dripped into a calcium lactate bath, calcium ions react with alginate molecules by allowing them to align and bind so that a thin gel membrane forms around the droplets. The gelification process that forms the membrane will stop the moment the sphere is rinsed, as its interior will be free of alginate molecules.

PREPARATION STEPS

01 Dissolve one sachet (2 g) of sodium alginate into 2 cups of the liquid ingredient.

N.B. THE USE OF A HAND BLENDER IS RECOMMENDED AS SOME EGG BEATERS WILL NOT BE POWERFUL ENOUGH.

02 Let the preparation sit for at least 15 minutes in order to allow the air bubbles trapped within the solution following the brewing of the preparation to escape.

N.B. TOO MANY AIR BUBBLES WILL CAUSE THE PREPARATION TO FLOAT WHEN DRIPPED INTO THE CALCIUM LACTATE BATH.

03 Prepare a calcium lactate bath by dissolving one sachet (5 g) of calcium lactate into 4 cups (1 l) of water.

04 Using a pipette, drip droplets of the preparation containing alginate molecules into the calcium lactate bath.

N.B. HOLD THE PIPETTE HORIZONTALLY, FROM A HEIGHT OF APPROXIMATELY 1 INCH, AND DRIP SLOWLY AND CONSTANTLY UNTIL THE PIPETTE IS EMPTIED.

05 Quickly collect the caviar from the calcium lactate bath using a slotted spoon or a sieve.

N.B. LEAVING THE CAVIAR TO SIT IN THE CALCIUM LACTATE BATH FOR MORE THAN 2 MINUTES WILL CAUSE ITS MEMBRANE TO THICKEN UNTIL THE CAVIAR IS COMPLETELY CONGEALED.

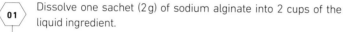

06 Rinse the caviar in cold water.

N.B. RINSING THE CAVIAR IS RECOMMENDED AS SOME CALCIUM MOLECULES MAY REMAIN ATTACHED TO IT, WHICH CAN CAUSE THE CAVIAR TO HAVE A BITTER AFTERTASTE. THE GELIFICATION PROCESS AS WELL AS THE THICKENING OF THE CAVIAR'S MEMBRANE WILL CONTINUE AFTER RINSING.

THE SOLUTION TO BE TRANSFORMED

Prepare about 2 cups of a solution to be spherified. The ingredient chosen must be very tasty, as the solution will lose some of its flavor when the sodium alginate is incorporated to it. An ingredient with high acidity will prevent the spherification process from being completed.

Warning: Any percentage of calcium in the ingredient will prevent the spherification process from being completed. The use of demineralized water is recommended, as tap water with a high calcium percentage could cause the sodium alginate solution to gelify.

SERVING AND PRESERVATION

For an optimal burst-in-the-mouth effect, serve within 15 minutes. Store the caviar in its original solution for a maximum of 12 hours before serving. The caviar will be completely congealed, but it should remain very tasty! The caviar can also be left to macerate in any other tasty solution to change its taste and color.

PLEASE NOTE

The interior of a caviar that is being exposed to calcium ions for too long will eventually end up completely congealed.

On the other hand, too short an exposition to calcium ions will cause the caviar's membrane to be too fragile and ultimately unable to maintain its shape.

REVERSE SPHERIFICATION

REVERSE SPHERIFICATION IS IDEAL TO ENCAPSULATE DENSER, THICKER LIQUIDS INTO A SPHERE THAT WILL BURST IN YOUR MOUTH! IT IS MAINLY USED TO SPHERIFY PUREES AND DAIRY PRODUCTS SUCH AS YOGURTS AND CREAMS. THE FROZEN VERSION OF THIS TECHNIQUE IS RECOMMENDED FOR A MORE LIQUID SPHERE INTERIOR.

PRINCIPLE

When a solution containing calcium lactate is submerged into a sodium alginate bath, calcium ions react with alginate molecules by allowing them to align and bind so that a thin gel membrane encapsulates the solution. The gelification process that forms the membrane will stop the moment the sphere is rinsed, as its interior will be free of alginate molecules.

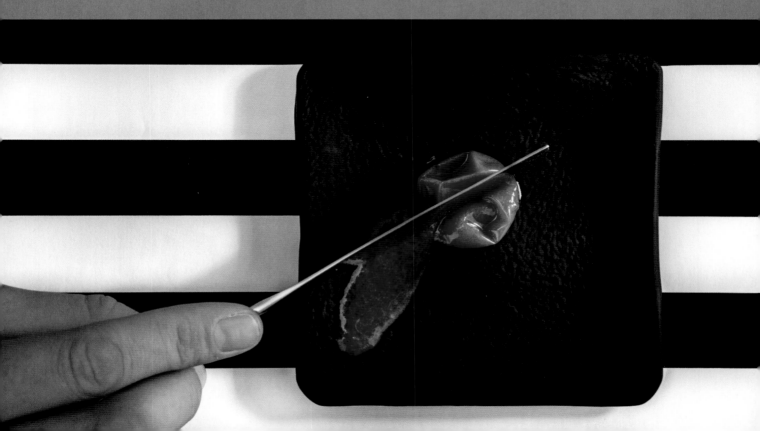

PREPARATION STEPS

01 Prepare the solution to be spherified so that it has a texture similar to that of a drinkable yogurt.

N.B.   OVERLY THICK INGREDIENTS CAN BE DILUTED WITH MILK OR WATER.

02 Dissolve a pinch of calcium lactate into the solution to be spherified.

N.B.   PRE-DISSOLVE CALCIUM SALTS IN A SMALL QUANTITY OF HOT WATER.

03 Prepare a sodium alginate bath in a flat-bottomed container by dissolving one sachet (2 g) of sodium alginate into 2 cups of water.

N.B.   THE USE OF A HAND BLENDER IS RECOMMENDED AS SOME EGG BEATERS WILL NOT BE POWERFUL ENOUGH.

04 Let the sodium alginate bath sit for at least 15 minutes to allow the air bubbles trapped within the solution following the brewing to escape.

N.B.   TOO MANY AIR BUBBLES WILL PREVENT THE CALCIUM IONS CONTAINED WITHIN THE FROZEN SPHERES FROM PIERCING THROUGH THE SURFACE OF THE SODIUM ALGINATE BATH.

05 Using a measuring spoon, submerge the preparation containing calcium ions into the sodium alginate bath.

N.B.   BRING THE SPOON CLOSE TO THE SODIUM ALGINATE BATH'S SURFACE THEN, GRADUALLY POUR ITS CONTENTS INTO THE BATH.

06 Let the calcium ions and alginate molecules interact for at least 3 minutes.

N.B.   DELICATELY TILT THE SPHERES IN THE SODIUM ALGINATE BATH IN ORDER TO ENSURE THAT THEIR MEMBRANE FORMS EVENLY

07 Collect the spheres from the sodium alginate bath using a slotted spoon and rinse them in cold water.

N.B.   THE GELIFICATION PROCESS WILL STOP THE MOMENT THE SPHERES ARE RINSED, AS THIS WILL STOP THE FORMATION OF THE MEMBRANE.

THE SOLUTION TO BE TRANSFORMED

Prepare about 1 cup of a solution to be spherified. The ingredient chosen must be quite dense. Fruit purees, creams and yogurts are recommended as they are very dense; thinner solutions will not penetrate the surface of the sodium alginate bath.

Warning: The use of demineralized water is recommended, as tap water with a high calcium percentage could cause the sodium alginate bath to gelify.

SERVING AND PRESERVATION

Store the spheres in their original solution for a maximum of 12 hours before serving.

To serve hot, let the spheres sit in hot water before serving.

Spheres can also be left to macerate in any other tasty solution to change the taste and color of their gel membrane.

PLEASE NOTE

Ensure that the spheres do not touch one another while in the bath as this can cause their membranes to stick together and eventually break.

Should the spheres' membrane break when manipulated, let the spheres rest for a longer time in the alginate bath in order to allow the membrane to gradually thicken.

REVERSE FROZEN SPHERIFICATION

REVERSE FROZEN SPHERIFICATION IS IDEAL TO ENCAPSULATE A WIDE RANGE OF LIQUIDS INTO A SPHERE THAT WILL BURST IN YOUR MOUTH! IT STANDS OUT MAINLY BECAUSE OF ITS GREAT VERSATILITY, AS IT ALLOWS YOU TO SPHERIFY CLEAR LIQUIDS SUCH AS ALCOHOLS AND ACIDIC JUICES SUCH AS LEMON JUICE.

PRINCIPLE

When a solution containing calcium lactate is submerged into a sodium alginate bath, calcium ions react with alginate molecules by allowing them to align and bind so that a thin gel membrane encapsulates the solution. The gelification process that forms the membrane will stop the moment the sphere is rinsed, as its interior will be free of alginate molecules.

PREPARATION STEPS

01 Dissolve a pinch of calcium lactate into the solution to be spherified.

N.B. IF SAID SOLUTION IS OF THE DENSER, THICKER VARIETY, PRE-DISSOLVE CALCIUM LACTATE INTO A SMALL QUANTITY OF WATER.

02 Pour the preparation into a mold and place it in the freezer until completely frozen.

N.B. EACH ICE CUBE WILL FORM A SPHERE. TOPPINGS SUCH AS SMALL PIECES OF FRUIT OR AROMATIC HERBS CAN BE PLACED IN THE MOLD BEFORE FREEZING.

03 Prepare a sodium alginate bath in a flat-bottomed container by dissolving one sachet (2 g) of sodium alginate into 2 cups of water.

N.B. THE USE OF A HAND BLENDER IS RECOMMENDED AS SOME EGG BEATERS WILL NOT BE POWERFUL ENOUGH.

04 Let the sodium alginate bath sit for at least 15 minutes to allow the air bubbles trapped within the solution following the brewing to escape.

N.B. TOO MANY AIR BUBBLES WILL PREVENT THE CALCIUM IONS CONTAINED WITHIN THE FROZEN SPHERES FROM PIERCING THROUGH THE SURFACE OF THE SODIUM ALGINATE BATH.

05 Submerge the frozen spheres containing calcium ions into the sodium alginate bath.

N.B. ENSURE THAT THE SPHERES DO NOT TOUCH ONE ANOTHER WHILE IN THE BATH BY STIRRING DELICATELY, AS THIS CAN CAUSE THEIR MEMBRANES TO STICK TOGETHER AND EVENTUALLY BREAK.

06 Let the calcium ions and alginate molecules interact for at least 3 minutes.

N.B. DELICATELY TILT THE SPHERES IN THE SODIUM ALGINATE BATH IN ORDER TO ENSURE THAT THEIR MEMBRANE FORMS EVENLY

07 Collect the spheres from the sodium alginate bath using a slotted spoon and rinse them in cold water.

N.B. THE GELIFICATION PROCESS WILL STOP THE MOMENT THE SPHERES ARE RINSED, AS THIS WILL STOP THE FORMATION OF THE MEMBRANE.

THE SOLUTION TO BE TRANSFORMED

Prepare about 1 cup of a solution to be spherified.

Toppings such as small pieces of fruit or aromatic herbs can be placed in the mold before freezing in order to remain encapsulated within the spheres.

The use of demineralized water is recommended, as tap water with a high calcium percentage could cause the sodium alginate bath to gelify.

Warning: Solutions with a high alcohol percentage cannot be frozen in a standard kitchen freezer, and neither can denser, thicker solutions such as honey-based or syrup-based solutions.

SERVING AND PRESERVATION

Store the spheres in their original solution for a maximum of 12 hours before serving.

To serve hot, let the spheres sit in hot water before serving.

Spheres can also be left to macerate in any other tasty solution to change the taste and color of their gel membrane.

PLEASE NOTE

Ensure that the spheres do not touch one another while in the bath as this can cause their membranes to stick together and eventually break.

Should the spheres' membrane break when manipulated, let the spheres rest for a longer time in the alginate bath in order to allow the membrane to gradually thicken.

SODIUM ALGINATE

NATURAL GELLING AGENT EXTRACTED FROM BROWN ALGAE OFTEN COMBINED WITH A CALCIUM SALT IN THE PROCESS OF SPHERIFICATION.

As you probably guessed, the name of this additive comes from its marine origin. In fact, sodium alginate is extracted from brown algae found on the coasts of the North Atlantic, Asia and South America. Its discovery was made by a chemist named E.C.C. Stanford, who described the molecule for the first time in 1881.

The food industry uses this algae extract in many different processes and, depending on the desired properties, manufacturers prefer several varieties of marine plants (Laminaria hyerborea, Laminaria digitata, Laminaria japonica, Ascophyllum nodosum, Ecklonia maxima).

Alginate is a polysaccharide, or a sugar chain, from the cell wall of algae. First extracted in the form of alginic acid, the product is then neutralized with salts that make it soluble and stable in a water solution. The solution goes through sifting, centrifuging and filtration before being precipitated in alginate salt.

Industry takes advantage of many of sodium alginate's properties. Its resistance to heat makes it an ingredient of choice in bakeries to make cream fillings or fruit jellies, allowing them to keep their shape during cooking. In addition, the thin film created around the gel or cream prevents it from affecting cake moisture. Its thickening effect in aqueous solutions is used to create thicker cheese sauces that adhere better to pasta. Alginate is also used as a stabilizer in ice cream by decreasing the size of crystals and obtaining a smoother texture. It also prevents the separation of emulsions such as salad dressings or mayonnaise. Gels form more easily when alginate is added to products with higher calcium concentrations.

DID YOU KNOW?

01

SODIUM ALGINATE re-shapes
chili pepper powder or pulp that
can then be used to stuff olives..

02

SODIUM ALGINATE is used
to make very reliable dental
impressions due to its fine
grain size.

03

SODIUM ALGINATE is used to
make replicas of human body
parts during filming of special
effects.

04

SODIUM ALGINATE is used to
make replicas of human body
parts during filming of special
effects.

CALCIUM LACTATE

CALCIUM SALT USED WITH SODIUM ALGINATE IN THE PROCESS OF SPHERIFICATION.

A salt is a compound derived from the joining of one positive ion (other than hydrogen H^+) with one negative ion (other than hydroxide OH^- ion). Ions can be metals (sodium, potassium), non-metals (carbon), acids (lactic acid) or bases, each providing either a positive or negative ion. Salts are usually very soluble in water.

Table salt, or sodium chloride, is well known for its flavor enhancing and preservative qualities, but in molecular gastronomy, calcium salts are used for gelling with sodium alginate.

Three calcium salts, derivatives of three acids (lactic, gluconic, chloric), are usually used in molecular gastronomy. However, calcium lactate is more popular, since it leaves no aftertaste, whereas calcium chloride leaves a certain bitterness in the mouth, even after rinsing the spheres with water.

The acid part of calcium lactate is derived from lactic acid, an acid available during the fermentation of sugars by lactobacilli bacteria. These same bacteria are needed to make yogurt, cheese and wine. For people with calcium deficiency, calcium lactate is one of the most recommended supplements due to its high absorption rates.

Calcium lactate is found in milk powder, but it is also used as a substrate for yeast in bakery products, an acidity stabilizer in baking powder, and a firming agent for grapefruit and canned peas.

DID YOU KNOW?

01

CALCIUM LACTATE increases
the remineralization of enamel
when added to chewing gum
containing xylitol.

02

CALCIUM LACTATE is found in
many aged cheeses, where it is
produced by bacteria during the
aging process.

03

CALCIUM LACTATE is used as
a firming agent for fresh-cut
fruits and vegetables as well as
processed fish to prevent the
degradation of their texture.

04

CALCIUM LACTATE is prescribed
to treat calcium deficiency and
osteoporosis.

EMULSIFICATION
DEFINITION AND TECHNIQUE

CREATE COLORFUL FOAMS THAT INTENSIFY AROMAS

EMULSIFICATION

CREATE COLORFUL FOAMS THAT INTENSIFY AROMAS.

What do chocolate, mayonnaise, salad dressing, milk, butter and ice cream have in common? All of them are emulsions!

The naked eye can only see a homogeneous product. However, this is not the case under the microscope, where thousands of small droplets dispersed in a second liquid substance can be seen. In each case, two substances that are normally immiscible, oil and water, have been mixed using an emulsifying agent.

An emulsion can also present the above-mentioned products in a different way. For example, a liquid can trap air bubbles and turn it into a foam. In molecular gastronomy, emulsification is the technique used to incorporate and stabilize air bubbles in a liquid mixture. It is possible to incorporate air bubble into a liquid simply by whisking vigorously. However, this phase is highly unstable and the air escapes in a relatively short time. To avoid this instability, an emulsifier can be incorporated into the solution.

Egg and milk protein, bread starch, gelatin and cream fat are common emulsifiers that have used in traditional cuisine for a long time. However, in recent decades, the food industry intensified its research in this field and discovered new emulsifiers such as soy lecithin and methylcellulose. These products are also called surfactants, a word derived from "surface active agents," since their molecules act as a barrier (interface) between water and air.

These additives bring great pleasure to molecular gastronomy enthusiasts by reducing the tension between the water and air surface, which stabilizes the air and foam. To better understand the forces at work, let's take a closer look at what happens inside air that is stabilized using soy lecithin.

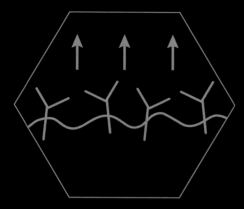

LECITHIN MOLECULE

The lecithin molecule looks like a hydrophilic pinhead, attracted by water, with two hydrophobic fatty acid legs that are repelled by water.

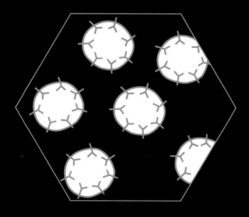

AIR BUBBLES FORMATION

The lecithin molecule positions itself around air bubbles, which inflate their hydrophilic portion towards the water. The air bubbles' surface is surrounded by lecithin molecules, thus preventing water from escaping from the liquid, which would deflate the foam.

OTHER CHARACTERISTICS

The secret of a successful foam is the amount of air bubbles dispersed in the liquid. In fact, a foam containing a larger number of small air bubbles is generally more stable than one formed using a small number of large bubbles.

So foam made with a whisk does not last as long as one made using a hand blender, since this powerful machine's cuts and re-cuts more air bubbles. A large amount of bubbles dispersed in the liquid also increases the viscosity of solutions, which gives foams their creaminess.

Although their viscosity increases the stability, foam and air remain relatively unstable; air bubbles gradually escape the liquid in which they were incorporated. Three main causes accelerate this phenomenon. First, the air can easily dissolve in liquids and evaporate. Next, the internal pressure of very tiny bubbles increases as their size decreases, eventually causing their membranes to burst. Finally, as there is a significant difference between the density of fluid and air, the two phases tend to separate, and liquid will gradually migrate to the bottom of the dish.

Finally, even when made using translucent ingredients, foams are always opaque. This unusual fact is explained by the many angles of light reflected on the walls of the air bubble. The light that is diffused in all directions thus creates the opacity and a certain brightness, depending on the color of the initial ingredients.

EMULSIFICATION

SOY LECITHIN IS USED TO TRANSFORM ANY LIQUID INTO A LIGHT AND TASTY FOAM.

PRINCIPLE

Soy lecithin is a natural protein contained in soy that has the unique property of stabilizing foam. This emulsifier is used to reach an unusal equilibrium between air and liquid. The foam will stand for about 30 minutes before it begins to dry, however the soy lecithin solution can be re-blended several times in order to obtain more foam.

PREPARATION STEPS

01 Dissolve one sachet (2 g) of soy lecithin into the solution to be lathered.

    N.B.   THE USE OF A HAND BLENDER IS RECOMMENDED AS SOME EGG BEATERS ARE NOT POWERFUL ENOUGH.

02 Incorporate as much air as possible into the soy lecithin preparation in order to produce foam.

    N.B.   HOLD THE HAND BLENDER AT AN ANGLE AND AVOID COMPLETELY IMMERSING ITS HEAD.

03 Collect foam and serve.

    N.B.   THE FOAM WILL HOLD FOR APPROXIMATELY 30 MINUTES BEFORE IT STARTS DRYING.

04 Reblend the soy lecithin preparation several times in order to obtain more foam.

THE SOLUTION TO BE TRANSFORMED

Prepare approximately 1⅓ cup (85 ml)s of a solution to be lathered and pour into a flat-bottomed container.

The solution to be spherified must contain a large proportion of water in order to favor the adherence of the lecithin molecules between the water and air bubbles.

Warning: Denser, thicker solutions such as honey-based or syrup-based solutions should be avoided, as the lecithin molecules do not contain enough water to retain the air bubbles.

SERVING AND PRESERVATION

The foam will hold for approximately 30 minutes before it starts drying.

Store the soy lecithin preparation in a closed container in the fridge for a few days if needed. Reblend the soy lecithin preparation several times in order to obtain more foam.

PLEASE NOTE

Soy lecithin is a natural protein contained in soy that has the unique property of stabilizing foam. This emulsifier is used to reach an unusal equilibrium between air and liquid. The foam will stand for about 30 minutes before it begins to dry, however the soy lecithin solution can be re-blended several times in order to obtain more foam.

SOY LECITHIN

NATURAL EMULSIFIER EXTRACTED FROM SOYBEAN, OFTEN USED TO SHAPE WATERY SOLUTIONS INTO AIRS.

Although you may not be aware of the usefulness of the lecithin molecule, your body knows very well how to use it! Lecithin is a constituent of cell membranes, specifically a phospholipid. It is like a hydrophilic pinhead with two hydrophobic fatty acid legs, which are essential properties for the formation of emulsions.

Besides cells in the human body, lecithin is mainly found in egg yolks, soybeans, liver, and wheat germ. The pharmacist Théodore Gobley isolated and described egg lecithin for the first time in 1847. Gobley gave it the name lekithos, the Greek word for egg yolk. He then spotted the group of molecules in many parts of animal bodies and in large quantities in the bile, blood and brain.

Lecithin found in eggs remains the most popular for making mayonnaise or hollandaise sauce, but industry usually extracts it from soy. During the manufacturing process, the soybean is first cooked, then crushed and finally precipitated by alcohol.

Lecithin is found in margarines and infant formula where it acts as an emulsifier. It is also found on the list of ingredients for ice preparations, such as sorbets and ice milk, where it allows fat to remain soluble in a high-water compound.

The body has the ability to manufacture lecithin, but if you want to use this product as a supplement, like fats, it provides the equivalent of 9 kilocalories per gram.

DID YOU KNOW?

01

SOY LECITHIN is incorporated
into many cosmetics to help
soften the skin and better
absorb other ingredients.

02

SOY LECITHIN is used as a
supplement in many types of
animal food, providing fat and
protein.

03

SOY LECITHIN enhances the
color and forms a protective
coating on painted surfaces
when added to paint.

04

SOY LECITHIN prevents food
from sticking to the bottom of
dishes and pans when added to
non-stick cooking sprays.

METHYLCELLULOSE

NATURAL EMULSIFIER DERIVED FROM CELLULOSE, USED TO CREATE DENSER FOAMS AND, WHEN EXPOSED TO HEAT, TO CREATE GELS THAT WILL MELT AS THEY COOL DOWN.

Derived from cellulose, a structural component of plant cells, methylcellulose was first introduced at the end of the 1930s in Germany, then a few years later in the United States. This extract from wood or cotton has several desirable characteristics such as film formation, water retention and the ability to form a gel with heat, which will melt upon cooling. It also acts as a thickening and binding agent.

Extraction of methylcellulose first requires mixing with an alkali, followed by the addition of methyl chloride, which transfers its methyl group to the molecule. The resulting pulp is then rinsed and filtered at a high temperature, so as to avoid gelling the product. Other cellulose by-products are also available on the market, such as hydroxypropyl methylcellulose (HPMC) and super methylcellulose (SMC).

Vegetable gum is soluble in cold water and forms a soft to firm elastic gel at temperatures around 122°F (50°C), although certain classes of the product can form a gel at about 86°F (30°C). When the temperature drops, the gel then returns to its original form as a solution. By heating, the molecule gets rid of its bonds with the water and forms new ones with its own kind, thus creating the structure needed for a gel. However, the addition of salt or sugar decreases the temperature at which the gel forms. The molecule also has hydrophobic characteristics and is able to trap air, which makes it the emulsifier of choice.

Methylcellulose is useful in the industry due to its stability during cooking and its ability to trap moisture and air, which increases the volume of dough and frozen dairy products. When added to French onions, it preserves the onion's shape and texture during cooking and reduces oil absorption by forming a film.

The ability of methylcellulose to preserve the shape of products makes it a popular ingredient in waffles and soy-based imitation meat. The presence of methylcellulose causes the formation of a gel during cooking, preventing the product from disintegrating, since it will be trapped by the gel. Once the food is cooled and the methylcellulose has returned to its soluble form, the gel disappears. No one will be any the wiser!

DID YOU KNOW?

01

METHYLCELLULOSE is calorie-free when ingested, as human digestive enzymes are unable to alter its molecules; the intestine does not retain it.

02

METHYLCELLULOSE is used in the composition of anti-constipation treatments due to its ability to absorb a lot of water during its passage through the digestive tract.

03

METHYLCELLULOSE is a main component in the manufacturing of fake semen used in the pornography industry.

04

METHYLCELLULOSE acts as a performance additive in concrete mixtures due to its properties that improve the product's viscosity and its adhesion to surfaces.

OTHER TRANSFOMATIONS
DEFINITION AND TECHNIQU

SIPHON WHIPPING, SUSPENSION, POWDERIZING, DEEP FREEZING

OTHER TRANSFORMATIONS

SIPHON WHIPPING, SUSPENSION, POWDERIZING, DEEP FREEZING.

Chefs who are passionate about molecular gastronomy adore innovating and experimenting. The modern cook's hardware is constantly expanding and culinary techniques are continually improving and being reinvented. Gelling, spherification and emulsification are the flagship techniques in molecular gastronomy. However, many other techniques are also used.

SIPHON WHIPPING

Siphon whipping differs from emulsification in that foams can be made without using an emulsifying agent. The product resulting from siphon whipping is usually called espuma, derived from the Spanish word for "foam".

The culinary whipper has been used for a long time to make Chantilly cream, also known as whipped cream. To do this, the cream is first poured into the siphon. Then an oxide nitrous (N2O) cartridge is inserted into the device, which releases its gas inside the bottle. Pressurized gas bubbles then penetrate the fatty liquid. This is why the cream's volume increases once the liquid has been ejected from the siphon. It is worth noting that the volume obtained is much greater than that achieved when using a whisk to make whipped cream.

Many espumas are made using liquid ingredients to which cream is added. Creams and other high-fat materials are always beneficial additions to espumas since fat molecules facilitate the dissolving of gas in the preparation. Solid ingredients can also be used, as long as the preparation is filtered before being transformed with the food siphon. Simply transform solid foods by cooking, then pureeing and extracting the juice using a fine sieve. Even very small particles may obstruct or clog the food siphon while it is pressurized.

Finally, emulsifiers or gelling agents can be substituted for cream fat. Additives such as gelatin, agar-agar or xanthan gum can help stabilize any kind of espuma – some may even be served hot! As with all recipes requiring hydrocolloids, we recommend letting the preparation settle a bit while the gas is pressurized in order to allow the molecules to hydrate. A settling period of 20 minutes inside the food siphon yields a much higher volume of an espuma compared with one in which the hydrocolloid does not have the time to properly hydrate.

SUSPENSION AND THICKENING

Thickening is not a new or spectacular culinary technique, but some thickening agents borrowed from the food processing industry are increasingly used in creative cuisine to add a slight touch of extravagance to dishes and cocktails! Without a doubt, xanthan gum is an additive that is becoming increasingly popular.

Due to its ability to replicate a creamy texture, xanthan gum is often used as a fat replacement in preparations. This creaminess is created by the bonds that join between the gum molecules, which form a network that traps air in the liquid preparation.

This same property is also used in molecular mixology whereby xanthan gum is added to cocktails to create a suspension effect. You can thus "suspend" fruit, herbs or flavor caviar in a liquid.

POWDERIZING

Another technique used in some recipes in this book is the transformation of liquids with high fat content into a fine powder. The additive that makes this technique possible is called maltodextrin and is derived from tapioca sugar, which comes in the form of a very low density powder.

The transformation into powder is a very straightforward process: simply add maltodextrin powder to a high-fat preparation and blend until you get the desired powdery texture. The solid ingredients must first be liquefied and it may be necessary to pass the powder through a sieve to remove any lumps.

So it's easy to add an entirely new dimension to dishes with a powder made from olive oil, chocolate, peanut butter or even bacon! By reducing the proportions of maltodextrin in the mixture, it is also possible to create flavored "lumps" that can be caramelized and crisped on the outside.

DEEP FREEZING

Liquid nitrogen has long been used in molecular gastronomy demonstrations and the instantaneous vapor cloud that results from the condensation of ambient air is very impressive.

However, besides its "wow" effect, there's another reason for this technique's enduring popularity. Due to its ability to quickly cool preparations, liquid nitrogen significantly outperforms the classic freezing process. Freezing at -4°F (-20°C) causes water to form into increasingly larger crystals and alters the product's initial structure. Frozen products thus lose a lot of their water and soften. The radical change in temperature brought about by nitrogen ensures the formation of much smaller ice crystals that leave the product's cell structure intact.

In cooking, liquid nitrogen is used as a coolant. It is not an ingredient and so it is never ingested; it cools the food, then evaporates. The food can be ingested only after the liquid nitrogen has fully evaporated. Foods that have been cooled with liquid nitrogen are extremely cold, as they have been in contact with this cryogenic substance, and should be left to warm up before being touched and ingested, in the same way that foods dipped in boiling oil must cool down before being touched. The denser the food, the colder it will be and therefore the longer it will need to warm up. This is why chefs usually dip low density confections, such as meringues or frozen mousse, into liquid nitrogen.

Some chefs use the cooling properties of liquid nitrogen to make extremely smooth ice cream. The creaminess of the ice cream is obtained due to the small size of the ice crystals formed during cooling with liquid nitrogen. Liquid nitrogen makes it possible to freeze alcohol to make original cocktails, which is not possible with traditional freezing techniques. It is also possible to create flavor powders using ingredients such as fruit or flowers that have been crushed when frozen.

However, the extreme cold of liquid nitrogen makes handling very dangerous. We recommend that you take training to understand the reactivity and risk of burns.

SIPHON WHIPPING

THERE IS MUCH MORE ONE CAN DO WITH A CULINARY WHIPPER THAN MAKE WHIPPED CREAM !

PRINCIPLE

A culinary whipper is designed to obtain a foamy mousse from a liquid by injecting gas into a closed flask containing the liquid and expelling it out under pressure. Siphons are available in several volumes (0,25L, 0,5L et 1L) and some can be used for hot preparations as well as cold ones.

Using food additives increases the number of ways a siphon can be used. For instance, xanthan gum can be used to replace the binding effect which is usually provided by the fat of cream to create an incredibly tasty low-fat whipped cream. Further, agar-agar allows the creation of warm mousses that can be served as appetizers or side dishes and cold soluble gelatin adds an exquisite melt-in-the-mouth effect to desserts !

PREPARATION STEPS

01 Pass the preparation through a sieve and fill the siphon.

> **N.B.** DO NOT FILL THE SIPHON COMPLETELY (MAXIMUM UP TO 3/4) AS THERE MUST BE ENOUGH ROOM FOR THE GAS. ONLY USE SOLUBLE INGREDIENTS. SOLID SUBSTANCES SUCH AS SEEDS AND PULP WILL CLOG THE DISCHARGING VALVE.

02 Close the siphon and insert an n2o gas cartridge.

> **N.B.** BEFORE LOADING A CARTRIDGE, MAKE SURE THAT THE LID IS TIGHTLY SEALED. A LIGHT HISSING SOUND INDICATE THAT THE CARTRIDGE HAS BEEN LOADED. USE ONE CARTRIDGE PER FILLING UNLESS OTHERWISE SPECIFIED IN THE RECIPE.

03 Hold the whipper vertically and shake briskly 4 or 5 times.

> **N.B.** ALWAYS SHAKE THE SIPHON IMMEDIATELY AFTER INSERTING THE GAS CARTRIDGE AND BEFORE EACH USE.

04 For cold preparations, refrigerate for at least 30 minutes.

> **N.B.** DEPENDING ON THE RECIPE, THE SIPHON MUST BE REFRIGERATED HORIZONTALLY FOR 30 MINUTES TO 2 HOURS.

05 For hot preparations, place in a hot water bath.

> **N.B.** HOT PREPARATIONS CAN SIT IN THE HOT WATER BATH OR BE SERVED AS SOON AS THE GAS IS INCORPORATED INTO THE PREPARATION. VERIFY THAT THE SIPHON IS HEAT RESISTANT. THE HOT WATER BATH MUST NOT EXCEED TEMPERATURES OF 120°F. USE A THERMOMETER TO KEEP TRACK OF THE TEMPERATURE.

06 To serve, hold the whipper upside down vertically and press lever Slowly and progressively.

> **N.B.** THE TRIGGER IS VERY SENSITIVE. TO AVOID CREATING A MESS, SLOWLY PRESS THE TRIGGER OVER THE SINK TO LET OUT A BIT OF AIR PRESSURE.

THE SOLUTION TO BE TRANSFORMED

Prepare roughly 1½ cups of preparation for a 500 ml siphon.

The solution to be whipped must contain either a fatty base like full-fat liquid cream, a gelifying base like agar-agar, gelatin, a supportive additive like xanthan gum or egg whites (not beaten). Depending on the doses and the more or less liquid consistency of the preparation poured into the siphon, the result will appear as anything from light and froth-like to solid whipped cream.

Warning: The siphon can easily become blocked. The preparation must absolutely be filtered through a very fine sieve before being poured into the siphon.

SERVING AND PRESERVATION

To keep its content fresh for several days, place the whipper in the refrigerator. To do so, remove the decorative nozzle, rinse it thoroughly and put it back on.

To serve warm espumas made out of **agar-agar**, mixtures can be warmed up directly in the culinary whipper by simply soaking the whipper in a bowl of hot water (158°F/ 70°C) before serving. Avoid putting a pressurised whipper directly on a hot burner or in boiling water.

Xanthan gum works like thousands of tiny sponges which is why it needs some time inside the whipper to hydrate before serving.

Cold soluble gelatin creates best results when used in cold recipes.

PLEASE NOTE

Do not open the whipper before pressure has completely escaped. Before removing the head, allow the remaining pressure to escape by pressing the lever.

Thoroughly clean each individual component with a mild detergent and a brush. It is particularly important to wash the head of the siphon to avoid any food residues to mildew and give a bad taste to the next preparations. The head is in general dismountable.

XANTHAN GUM

NATURAL THICKENER DERIVED FROM GLUCOSE VIA FERMENTATION, OFTEN USED TO STABILIZE EMULSIONS AND THICKEN SAUCES AND DRINKS.

Derived from a fermentation process by bacteria, xanthan gum was discovered in the 1950s by American scientists. The microorganism Xanthomonas Campestri transforms sugars, nitrogen, magnesium and other minerals into polysaccharides. This transformation is a little like yeast which, when combined with sugars, produces alcohol and carbon dioxide.

These micro-organisms occur naturally on plants in the cabbage family and they are often responsible for the presence of dark spots on broccoli, cauliflower and other leafy vegetables. In factories, the bacteria are inoculated in a sterile environment until their fermentation has finished. The microorganisms are finally eliminated by heat and the gum is collected through precipitation, centrifuging and drying.

Xanthan gum belongs to the hydrocolloid family, and like each member of this family, its molecules must have time to hydrate after having been dissolved. This hydration period allows water to penetrate inside hydrocolloid molecules, which then facilitate reactions as they are surrounded by water and suspended in the solvent. Hydration can be done equally well in a hot or cold liquid.

Heat only slightly alters the thickening effect of xanthan gum once the product has cooled, but its viscosity is temporarily decreased during the process. This additive also tolerates a wide range of pH and the presence of salts and alcohol up to 60%, but it is best to complete the hydration phase before these additions.

Xanthan gum is a thickener and stabilizer, but it does not form a gel. Rather, it suspends particles in salad dressings and gives sauces their creamy texture. By preventing bread starches from crystallizing, it also preserves freshness. For this reason, it is commonly used in bakeries.

Pseudoplasticity is also a property of xanthan gum widely used by the industry. It consists in the ability of a preparation to change from a thick, viscous form to an almost liquid state after stirring. A dressing containing xanthan gum will thus be thick when the bottle is slowly turned upside down, but its contents become liquid if the bottle is vigorously shaken before being turned upside down. It returns to its original viscosity when put back to rest.

Fifty percent of xanthan gum is used outside the food industry, including cosmetics, personal hygiene products, and the pharmaceutical industry, where it is also used as a stabilizer.

DID YOU KNOW?

01

Xanthan gum causes a
noticeable increase in viscosity
at concentrations as low as 1%.

02

Xanthan gum prevents the
formation of ice crystals in
ice cream and increases the
moisture and volume of gluten-
free bakery products.

03

Xanthan gum provides a high
fat mouth feel in many light
sauces, milk shakes and dips.

04

Xanthan gum is a common
ingredient in fake blood recipes.

MALTODEXTRIN

UNSWEET SUGAR MOSTLY USED IN CREATIVE COOKING AS AN AROMA CARRIER, IN THE FORM OF TASTY POWDER THAT CAN BE SPRINKLED OVER FOOD PREPARATIONS AND DISHES.

Maltodextrin is derived from starch from grains such as corn or rice, tubers such as potatoes, or roots such as tapioca. This starch is composed of long chains of sugar and is the plant's food reserve.

Once the starch is extracted from the original product, it is hydrolyzed, that is, degraded by enzymes. The process is virtually the same as in starch degradation by enzymes in the digestive system.

Although the composition of maltodextrin is a blend of sugar, its sweetening power is much weaker than that of syrups and table sugar! The indicator used to measure the hydrolysis degree of sugars is called "Dextrose Equivalent" (DE). DE ranges from 0 to 100 where 0 corresponds to untransformed starch and 100 corresponds to simple dextrose molecules, i.e., entirely hydrolyzed sugar. On this scale, refined sugar of the type generally used in cooking occupies the 92 to 99 range. Syrups, such as corn syrup, have a DE between 20 and 91. Maltodextrins have a DE below 20, so they range between starch and syrups.

In the food industry, maltodextrin is used to make soft, low-fat bakery products. It also prevents the formation of crystals on the surface of frozen foods and is used as a sugar substrate in sports drinks.

Besides the food sector, its uses are diverse. Some soaps use it as an aroma carrier and texturizer. The pharmaceutical industry uses its properties to reduce crystallization in syrups and as a filler in tablets.

The use of maltodextrin has been further extended in molecular gastronomy by absorbing fats to create flavorful powder. Since maltodextrin is easily soluble in water – and therefore in the saliva – once in the mouth, these powders melt and release their fat.

DID YOU KNOW?

01

Maltodextrin is added to beer to improve its mouthfeel.

02

Maltodextrin is a significant part of the content of powdered energy drinks used by athletes.

03

Maltodextrin is used in the manufacturing of many drugs to improve taste, shape or solubility.

04

Maltodextrin is considered by nutritionists to be an empty substance containing virtually no calories, vitamins or nutrients.

LIQUID NITROGEN

A MAJOR COMPONENT OF AIR USED IN ITS LIQUID FORM TO CREATE THE SMOOTHEST ICE CREAM AND COOK WITH THE COLD.

It was not until the 19th century that scientists managed to liquefy gases by cooling them to extreme temperatures.

Nowadays, the usefulness of such processes is undeniable, and it is now impossible to visit a hospital without coming face-to-face with a liquid oxygen tank. Liquid nitrogen is also widely used in this environment to conserve body fluids such as blood or sperm, in addition to eliminating potentially malignant skin lesions such as warts.

Chef Heston Blumenthal introduced liquid nitrogen to the world of molecular gastronomy through Peter Barham, a physics professor and author of the book "The Science of Cooking." In the early 2000s, the chef of the restaurant "Fat Duck" in the United Kingdom served a foam cryogenized with liquid nitrogen from start to finish in front of his clients.

One must always exercise great caution when handling liquid nitrogen. The gas maintained in a liquid state at a temperature of -321°F (-196°C) tries to escape and evaporate. It must be carefully carried in containers provided for this purpose, such as Dewar flasks, double-wall insulated vessels designed for liquefied gases. Keeping liquid nitrogen in an airtight container would turn it into a real pressure bomb! Liquid nitrogen can also cause serious cold burns. In addition, if it is used in a poorly ventilated room, it can cause asphyxiation. The expression "handle with care" therefore makes sense!

DID YOU KNOW?

01

Liquid nitrogen is produced directly from ambient air liquefied after distillation separates its various components.

02

Liquid nitrogen has been used since 1902 as a source of energy to propel a cryogenic motor vehicle.

03

Liquid nitrogen is the basis for a new concept in ecological funerals whereby the corpse is dipped in liquid nitrogen and then turned into fine particles.

04

Liquid nitrogen is used to cool certain materials to produce a state of superconductivity.

MOLECULAR
50 COURSE MEAL

CAVIAR &
CHAMPAGNE

INGREDIENTS

APRICOT CAVIAR

1 ½ cups (375 ml) apricot juice
2 cups (500 ml) water
1 sachet (2 g) SODIUM ALGINATE
1 sachet (5 g) CALCIUM LACTATE

STRAWBERRY CAVIAR

1 ⅓ cups (335 ml) lukewarm water
5 tbs (75 ml) strawberry jam
1 tbs (15 ml) cane sugar
2 cups (500 ml) water
1 sachet (2 g) SODIUM ALGINATE
1 sachet (5 g) CALCIUM LACTATE

TO SERVE

Champagne or other sparkling wine

DIRECTIONS

APRICOT CAVIAR*

01 In a rectangular, flat-bottomed bowl and using a hand blender, dissolve 1 sachet of SODIUM ALGINATE in apricot juice. Let sit for 10 minutes.

02 Dissolve 1 sachet of CALCIUM LACTATE in 2 cups (500 ml) of water using a spoon. Then, using a pipette held at a 90° angle, slowly drip droplets of the alginate solution into the calcium lactate bath. Let sit for 3 minutes, then empty the calcium lactate bath into the sink and onto a sieve so you're left with just the apricot caviar. Rinse in lukewarm water.

STRAWBERRY CAVIAR*

03 In a rectangular, flat-bottomed bowl and using a hand blender, dissolve 1 sachet of SODIUM ALGINATE in lukewarm water, jam and sugar. Let sit for 10 minutes.

04 Dissolve 1 sachet of CALCIUM LACTATE in 2 cups (500 ml) of water using a spoon. Then, using a pipette held at a 90° angle, slowly drip droplets of the alginate solution into the calcium lactate bath. Let sit for 3 minutes, then empty the calcium lactate bath into the sink and onto a sieve so you're left with just the strawberry caviar. Rinse in lukewarm water.

ASSEMBLY

05 Fill champagne glasses with sparkling wine, then place a few pearls in each glass. Serve.

VOLATILE AMUSE-BOUCHE

DIFFICULTY   3/5
ACTIVE TIME   1:20
TOTAL TIME   2:20
*TIPS ON PEARLS   P. 22

INGREDIENTS

tall glass of oil

CROSTINI

1 baguette
½ cup (125 ml) salted butter
2 tbs (30 ml) chives
¼ tsp (1.25 ml) ground white pepper
¼ tsp (1.25 ml) onion powder
1 tsp (5 ml) chopped parsley
sea salt, to taste

CRANBERRY PEARLS

1 ¼ cups (315 ml) pure cranberry juice
2 tbs (30 ml) maple syrup
1 sachet (2 g) AGAR-AGAR

TO SERVE

8 slices goat cheese
8 tarragon leaves
basil aroma by MOLECULE-R

DIRECTIONS

 01 Refrigerate oil to cool overnight, or, to save time, place it in the freezer for 1 hour.

CROSTINI

 02 Preheat oven to 300 °F (150 °C). Slice 8 croutons off of the baguette and place them on a lightly oiled baking sheet. Finely chop chives.

 03 Melt butter in a pan. Add in chives, parsley, onion powder, salt and pepper and mix well. Brush croutons on both sides with chives butter and cook in the oven for 6 minutes (turn halfway through cooking time) or until crisp.

CRANBERRY **PEARLS***

 04 In a pot, reduce cranberry juice to 1 cup. Add in AGAR-AGAR and maple syrup. Bring to a boil, then remove from heat immediately.

 05 Remove oil from the freezer or refrigerator. Using a pipette held at a 90° angle, slowly drip droplets of the agar-agar preparation in the cold oil. Pour onto a sieve and above the sink to get rid of the oil and rinse under cold water. Set aside.

ASSEMBLY

 06 Drip a droplet or two of basil aroma onto a piece of blotting paper inserted in an AROMASPOON™ by MOLECULE-R. In the spoon, place a piece of crostini topped with cranberry pearls, a piece of goat cheese and a tarragon leave, and repeat with the rest of the crostini. When taking a bite, keep the AROMASPOON close to your nose while chewing. Inhale the basil aroma and experience volatile flavoring!

DEEP-FROZEN GIN & TONIC

DIFFICULTY   1/5
ACTIVE TIME   0:05
TOTAL TIME   0:05

INGREDIENTS

1 tbs (15 ml) grapefruit juice
1 rosemary sprig
grapefruit zest
2 fl oz (60 ml) gin
tonic water, to taste
dry ice

NOTE

The above quantities are for 1 serving.
Double, triple or quadruple as needed.

DIRECTIONS

01   Place a piece of dry ice at the bottom of a glass.

02   Add rosemary sprig, zest, grapefruit juice, gin, and finally soda, and serve.

VODKA DICE
& GAZPACHO

DIFFICULTY   3/5
ACTIVE TIME   0:10
TOTAL TIME   1:10

INGREDIENTS

VODKA DICE

1 cup (250 ml) vodka
1 tbs (15 ml) white sugar
1 green onion
1 sachet (2 g) AGAR-AGAR

GAZPACHO

2 cups (500 ml) tomato juice
2 blanched tomatoes
1 cucumber
1 roasted red bell pepper
1 white onion
1 garlic clove
¾ cup (190 ml) watermelon
1 tbs (15 ml) balsamic vinegar
1 tbs (15 ml) olive oil
salt and pepper, to taste

DIRECTIONS

GAZPACHO

 Peel and seed tomatoes and cucumber. Dice tomatoes and cut cucumber into a brunoise. Peel and dice pepper, dice onion and finely chop garlic. Seed watermelon and cut it into a brunoise as well. Reserve 2 tbs brunoised cucumber and 1 tbs brunoised watermelon for garnish.

 Combine all ingredients in a blender until smooth and homogenous. Refrigerate for 1 hour. (Make vodka dice while you wait.)

VODKA DICE

 Finely chop green onion. In a pot, bring vodka and sugar to a boil with 1 sachet AGAR-AGAR, then remove from heat immediately. Stir in green onion and pour into a rectangular plastic container. Refrigerate for 30 minutes. Unmold and cut into a very small dice.

ASSEMBLY

 Divide vodka dice and gazpacho between serving spoons. Top with brunoised cucumber and watermelon.

VOLATILE LAMB AMUSE-BOUCHE

DIFFICULTY	1/5
ACTIVE TIME	0:45
TOTAL TIME	0:45
*TIPS ON FOAM	P. 56

INGREDIENTS

1 big bunch rosemary

ROASTED VEGETABLES

2 tbs (30 ml) olive oil
1 onion
2 red bell peppers
2 zucchinis
salt, to taste
pepper, to taste

ROSEMARY FOAM

2 tbs (30 ml) lemon juice
1 ½ cups (375 ml) water
1 sachet (2 g) SOY LECITHIN

LAMB

2 lbs (900 g) lamb noisettes
all-purpose flour
1 tbs (15 ml) olive oil
2 tbs (30 ml) butter
½ cup (125 ml) dry white wine
1 tbs (15 ml) Dijon mustard
1 cup (250 ml) heavy cream

TO SERVE

smoke aroma by MOLECULE-R

DIRECTIONS

ROASTED VEGETABLES

 01 Preheat oven to 375 °F (190 °C). Line 2 baking sheets (or 1 large baking sheet) with tin foil. Coarsely chop onion and bell pepper. Slice zucchini into ⅔-of-an-inch-thick (2 cm) discs.

 02 Place prepped vegetables on baking sheet. Drizzle with olive oil, season with salt and pepper and toss to coat. Top with a few rosemary sprigs. Make sure vegetables are as spread out as possible on the baking sheet. Cook for 40 minutes, tossing twice. (While you wait, make rosemary foam and lamb.)

ROSEMARY **FOAM***

 03 Infuse remaining rosemary in water (save 2 sprigs for the last part of the recipe), on low heat, for 15 minutes. Remove sprigs and filter through a sieve. Let sit to cool.

 04 In a rectangular, flat-bottomed bowl, combine rosemary infusion and lemon juice and sprinkle in SOY LECITHIN. Using a hand blender, blend for 3 to 4 minutes, then let sit for 5 minutes. To serve, collect foam using a spoon. If needed and to obtain more foam, repeat this step.

LAMB

 05 Season lamb noisettes with salt and pepper and cover in a thin layer of flour. Sauté for 2 to 3 minutes, in a pan, with oil and butter. Remove noisettes from pan and reserve, covered.

 06 Deglaze pan with white wine. Add in the last 2 rosemary sprigs and simmer for 3 minutes. Incorporate mustard and cream and remove from heat. Place noisettes back in the pan and coat them with sauce. Serve immediately.

ASSEMBLY

 07 Cut the noisettes into small pieces. Drip a droplet or two of smoke aroma onto a piece of blotting paper inserted in an AROMAFORK™ by MOLECULE-R. In the fork, place a piece of noisette and some roasted vegetables, and top with rosemary foam. When taking a bite, keep the AROMASPOON close to your nose while chewing. Inhale the smoke aroma and experience volatile flavoring!

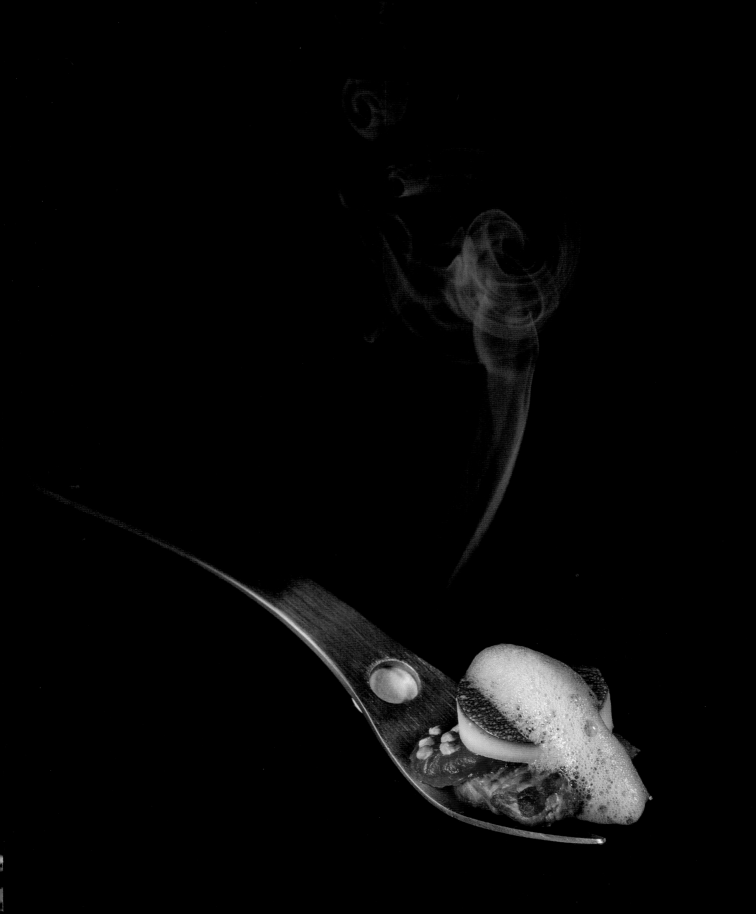

NOUVEAU GENRE
PANNA COTTA

DIFFICULTY	2/5
ACTIVE TIME	0:45
TOTAL TIME	0:45
*TIPS ON CAVIAR	P. 42

INGREDIENTS

GREEN PEA PUREE

28 oz (800 g) frozen green peas
1 bunch lemon basil
2 cups (500 ml) heavy cream
salt, to taste
pepper, to taste

BASIL CAVIAR

1 bunch lemon basil, chopped
2 cups (500 ml) pea water (from the puree)
1 tbs (15 ml) ground pepper
2 cups (500 ml) water
1 sachet (2 g) SODIUM ALGINATE
1 sachet (5 g) CALCIUM LACTATE

PEA SHOTS

1⅓ cups (335 ml) green pea puree
1 sachet (2 g) AGAR-AGAR

GARNISH

1 tsp (5 ml) butter
½ tsp (2.5 ml) salt
pepper

TO SERVE

a few chive sprigs
¼ cup (65 ml) coconut shavings
1 carrot

DIRECTIONS

GREEN PEA PUREE

01 Cook green peas for 10 minutes in lots of salted boiling water, then drain. Reserve ¼ cup (65 ml) cooked peas for garnish. Reserve the pea water.

02 Chop basil. In a food processor, combine basil, peas and cream until smooth and homogenous. Pass through a chinois or a sieve to get rid of any lumps. Reserve.

BASIL CAVIAR*

03 In a pan, on low heat, let the basil infuse in 2 cups (500 ml) of pea water for 5 minutes. Remove from heat. Remove the basil, add the red pepper and immediately, using a hand blender, dissolve 1 sachet of SODIUM ALGINATE in the basil infusion. Let sit for 20 minutes.

04 Dissolve 1 sachet of CALCIUM LACTATE in 2 cups (500 ml) of water using a spoon. Then, using a pipette held at a 90° angle, slowly drip droplets of the alginate solution into the calcium lactate bath. Let sit for 3 minutes, then empty the calcium lactate bath into the sink and onto a sieve so you're left with just the apricot caviar. Rinse in lukewarm water.

PEA SHOTS

05 Bring 1⅓ cups (335 ml) of green pea puree to a boil with AGAR-AGAR (reserve the remainder), then remove from heat immediately. Pour mixture into shot glasses and let sit for 20 minutes in the refrigerator.

06 Unmold pea shots and use a knife to diagonally cut the base (see picture). Using a small spoon, dig into each shot to make as much room as possible for garnish while leaving an ⅛ inch (5 mm) rim. Reserve at room temperature.

GARNISH

07 Preheat oven to 350 °F (175 °C). In a pan, on medium heat, warm up reserved peas in butter with salt and pepper. Place coconut shavings on a baking sheet and bake in oven for 3-4 minutes.

ASSEMBLY

08 Warm remaining pea puree on the stove. While you wait, chop chives and use a mandoline to cut long carrot slices. Fill pea shots with warm puree, top with whole peas, coconut shavings and chives, and arrange carrot slices so they look like the handle of a cup.

DECONSTRUCTED MISO

DIFFICULTY   3/5
ACTIVE TIME   0:40
TOTAL TIME   1:00
*TIPS ON SPAGHETTIS P. 24
*TIPS ON FOAM   P. 56

INGREDIENTS

MISO SOUP

1 oz (30 g) dried shiitakes
1 cup (250 ml) water
1 cup (250 ml) white mushrooms
2 cups (500 ml) vegetable broth
4 lemongrass stalks
½ bunch cilantro
¼ cup (65 ml) soy sauce
2 tbs (30 ml) miso
6 green onions
4 slices ginger root
⅛ oz (5 g) dried wakame
1 tbs (15 ml) butter
a dash sesame oil
salt and pepper to taste

MISO SPAGHETTIS

¾ cup (190 ml) miso soup, filtered
4 cups (1l) ice cubes
1 sachet (2 g) AGAR-AGAR

LEMONGRASS & CILANTRO FOAM

1 cup (250 ml) water
1 bunch cilantro
6 lemongrass stalks
2 tbs (30 ml) lime juice
1 sachet (2 g) SOY LECITHIN

TO SERVE

blue-foot muhrooms
enoki muhrooms
fresh wakame

DIRECTIONS

MISO SOUP

01 Bring water to a boil. Remove water from heat, then add in shiitakes. Rehydrate for 15 minutes. While you wait, coarsely chop white mushrooms, green onions, lemongrass and cilantro. Reserve both the shiitakes and steepwater.

02 In a large pan, sauté the white mushrooms with butter until their water evaporates. Season with salt and pepper. Add in the shiitakes, green onions and sesame oil, then cook for 2 more minutes. Add in the steepwater and vegetable broth and bring to a boil. Finally, lower heat, add in lemongrass, cilantro, soy sauce, wakame and ginger, and simmer for 20 minutes, stirring occasionally. (Start making LEMONGRASS & CILANTRO FOAM while you wait.)

03 Once soup has reduced a bit, turn off the heat and stir in miso. Filter and discard solids.

MISO SPAGHETTIS*

04 Place ice cubes in a large bowl and fill with cold water.

05 Bring ¾ of a cup (190 ml) of filtered miso soup to a boil with AGAR-AGAR, then remove from heat immediately.

06 Fill a food grade syringe with the agar-agar preparation. Plug syringe into a silicone tube and fill up the tube, then place it in the ice bath for 1 minute. Remove the tube from the ice bath, then, using the syringe again, push air into the tube to eject the spaghetti. Repeat until enough spaghettis are obtained.

LEMONGRASS & CILANTRO FOAM*

07 Bring water to a boil. While you wait, coarsely chop cilantro and lemongrass. Remove boiling water from heat and infuse cilantro and lemongrass for 10 minutes. Add in lime juice and let sit to cool.

08 Transfer cooled infusion to a rectangular, flat-bottomed bowl. Sprinkle in SOY LECITHIN. Using a hand blender, blend for 3 to 4 minutes, then let sit for 5 minutes.

09 To serve, collect foam using a spoon. If needed and to obtain more foam, repeat step 8.

ASSEMBLY

10 Divide spaghettis between plates and decorate each plate with blue-foot mushrooms, enoki mushrooms and wakame. Serve lemongrass and cilantro foam on the side.

DECONSTRUCTED
CLAM RISOTTO

INGREDIENTS

CLAM-FLAVORED SPAGHETTIS

¾ cup (190 ml) canned clam juice
¼ cup (65 ml) soy sauce
4 cups (1 l) ice cubes
1 sachet (2 g) AGAR-AGAR

CLAM SAUCE

2 tbs (30ml) butter
1 shallot, chopped
½ clove garlic
¼ cup (65 ml) white wine
1 cup (250 ml) canned clams with juice
½ cup (125 ml) 35% cooking cream
salt, to taste
pepper, to taste

DIRECTIONS

CLAM-FLAVORED **SPAGHETTIS***

 01 Place ice cubes in a large bowl and fill with cold water.

 02 Bring the canned clam juice, soy sauce and AGAR-AGAR to a boil and stir for 2 minutes.

 03 Fill a food grade syringe with the agar-agar preparation. Plug syringe into a silicone tube and fill up the tube, then place it in the ice bath for 1 minute. Remove the tube from the ice bath, then, using the syringe again, push air into the tube to eject the spaghetti. Repeat until enough spaghettis are obtained.

CLAM SAUCE

04 Melt the butter in a pan and brown the shallot and garlic. Deglaze with white wine and reduce.

05 Add the clam juice from the canned clams to the pan and bring to a boil. Add the clams and cream. Season with salt and pepper and cook for 2 minutes.

ASSEMBLY

06 Chop the spaghettis slantwise into rice-shaped pieces. Serve the clam-flavored rice on a plate coated with clam sauce.

DECONSTRUCTED CASSEROLE

INGREDIENTS

1 tall glass filled with oil

MUSHROOM BROTH

½ oz (15 g) dried mushrooms
1 cup (250 ml) boiling water
2 tbs (30 ml) olive oil
2 cups (500 ml) cremini mushrooms
6 green onions
3 cups (750 ml) chicken broth
3 thyme sprigs
salt and pepper, to taste

POTATO PAPILLOTTE

4 potatoes
¼ cup (65 ml) olive oil
1 tsp (5 ml) smoked paprika
1 tsp (5 ml) garlic powder
salt and pepper, to taste

PARMESAN TILES

½ cup (125 ml) grated parmesan

SPINACH WITH GARLIC & PARMESAN

2 cups (500ml) fresh spinach
1 garlic clove
¼ cup (65 ml) grated parmesan
2 tbs (30 ml) butter
salt and pepper, to taste

FRIED CHERRY TOMATOES

12 cherry tomatoes
lots of peanut or sunflower oil
sea salt, to taste
Espelette pepper

SALTED HERB PEARLS

½ cup (125 ml) milk
½ cup (125 ml) water
garden herbs
2 tsp (10 ml) sea salt
1 sachet (2 g) AGAR-AGAR

TO SERVE

cubed feta
chives

NOTE

You may use any combination of sage, thyme, rosemary, oregano, marjoram or basil as garden herbs.

DIRECTIONS

01 Refrigerate oil to cool overnight, or, to save time, place it in the freezer for 1 hour.

MUSHROOM BROTH

02 Rinse dried mushrooms and place them in a bowl. Add them in boiling water and let soak for 15 minutes (slice cremini mushrooms and coarsely chop green onions while you wait), then drain (save both steepwater and mushrooms) using a piece of cheese cloth and chop coarsely.

03 Heat oil on medium heat in a pot. Sauté creminis and green onions for 5 minutes or until all liquid has evaporated. Add in chicken broth, rehydrated mushrooms, steepwater and thyme, then bring to a boil. Reduce heat and simmer for 40 minutes (Make POTATO PAPILLOTE while you wait). When done, season and drain to discard all solids.

POTATO PAPILLOTTE

04 Preheat oven to 350 °F (175 °C) and dice potatoes. Combine all other ingredients, transfer to a resealable plastic bag and add in potato dice. Shake well to coat.

05 Wrap potatoes in tin foil, papillote-style, and cook in the oven for 30 minutes (Make PARMESAN TILES while you wait). Stir halfway through cooking time.

PARMESAN TILES

06 Once the potatoes are in the oven, line a baking sheet with parchment paper. On it, place 6 small handfuls of grated parmesan and spread into circles. Cook in the oven for 8 to 10 minutes, until golden, then carefully transfer to a plate lined with paper towels.

SPINACH WITH GARLIC & PARMESAN

07 Finely chop garlic. In a large pan, sauté garlic in butter. Add in spinach and wilt on high heat until all water has evaporated. Remove from heat and incorporate parmesan. Season, cover and reserve.

FRIED CHERRY TOMATOES

08 Prepare a deep-fryer, or alternatively, fill a pot with oil and bring to a temperature of 350 °F (175 °C). Place tomatoes in oil and fry until the skin comes off (this will happen quickly). Season with salt and Espelette pepper.

SALTED HERB **PEARLS***

09 Infuse herbs in water on low heat for 20 minutes. Filter (discard herbs) and add in milk, salt and AGAR-AGAR. Bring to a boil, then remove from heat immediately.

10 Remove oil from the freezer or refrigerator. Using a pipette held at a 90° angle, slowly drip droplets of the agar-agar preparation in the cold oil. Pour onto a sieve and above the sink to get rid of the oil and rinse under cold water. Set aside.

ASSEMBLY

11 Serve in hollow plates. Using a round or square cookie cutter, layer as follows: potato dice, spinach, tomatoes. Remove cutter and top with a parmesan tile. Add in pearls, chives and feta cubes as pictured and finish with a ladleful or mushroom broth.

MODERN
SPRING TARTARE

DIFFICULTY   2/5
TOTAL TIME   0:45
ACTIVE TIME   1:45
*TIPS ON PEARLS   P. 22
*TIPS ON FOAM   P. 56

INGREDIENTS

1 tall glass filled with oil

YUZU PEARLS

¾ cup (190 ml) yuzu juice
1 tbs (15 ml) honey
1 tbs (15 ml) water
1 sachet (2 g) AGAR-AGAR

CRISPY QUINOA

⅔ cup (170 ml) black quinoa
1 cup (250 ml) peanut oil

CILANTRO FOAM

1 bunch cilantro
1 ⅔ cups (415 ml) water
1 sachet (2 g) SOY LECITHIN

AVOCADO TARTARE

4 ripe avocados
12 chive stems
4 tbs mayonnaise
1 tsp (5 ml) toasted sesame oil
1 tsp (5 ml) yuzu juice
salt and pepper to taste

DIRECTIONS

01 Refrigerate oil until very cold, or, to save time, place it in the freezer for 1 hour.

YUZU **PEARLS***

02 In a pot, combine yuzu juice, honey and water. Sprinkle in AGAR-AGAR and mix it in using a spoon. Bring to a boil, then remove from heat immediately.

03 Remove the cold oil from the freezer or refrigerator. Using a pipette held at a 90° angle, slowly drip droplets of the agar-agar preparation into the cold oil. Stir gently, then, using a sieve, collect pearls and briefly rinse them under water. Reserve.

CRISPY QUINOA

04 Cook quinoa according to package instructions. (While the quinoa is cooking, save time by doing step 6 of CILANTRO FOAM.)

05 In a pan, heat peanut oil on medium heat and stir in cooked quinoa. Cook while stirring for 4-5 minutes, then remove from heat and reserve.

CILANTRO **FOAM***

06 Chop cilantro (reserve a few leaves for garnish), then place it in a pot with water. Infuse on low heat for 15 minutes, then let sit 15 more minutes to cool down.

07 Once cilantro infusion has cooled down, drain using a sieve (discard cilantro leaves) and transfer liquid to a rectangular, flat-bottomed bowl. Sprinkle in SOY LECITHIN. Using a hand blender, blend for 3 to 4 minutes, then let sit for 5 minutes.

08 To serve, collect foam using a spoon. If needed and to obtain more foam, repeat step 7.

AVOCADO TARTARE

09 Dice avocados and chop chives finely. Then, combine with other tartare ingredients in a bowl. Make sure you do this shortly before serving, as the avocado will oxidize otherwise.

ASSEMBLY

10 Divide quinoa and tartare between ramekins, then top each one with cilantro foam, yuzu pearls and one or two cilantro leaves.

KALE CLOUD
& BEET TARTARE

DIFFICULTY   2/5
ACTIVE TIME   0:20
TOTAL TIME   0:20
*TIPS ON FOAM   P. 56

INGREDIENTS

BEET TARTARE

2 cups (500 ml) cooked beets
2 red onions
4 tbs (60 ml) capers
10 dill pickles
1 bunch tarragon
1 tbs (15 ml) mayonnaise
1 tbs (15 ml) whole grain mustard
2 tbs (30 ml) Yorkshire sauce
raspberry vinegar to taste
salt and pepper to taste

APPLE & KALE FOAM

2 apples
½ bunch kale
1 celery rib
1 sachet (2 g) SOY LECITHIN

TO GARNISH

caperberries
edible flowers

DIRECTIONS

BEET TARTARE

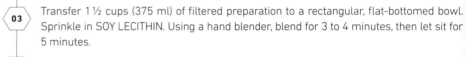

01   Finely dice beets, then combine with other tartare ingredients and set aside.

APPLE & KALE FOAM*

02   Chop apples, kale and celery. Then, using a cold press juicer, extract juices and drain using a sieve to get rid of any clumps.

03   Transfer 1 ½ cups (375 ml) of filtered preparation to a rectangular, flat-bottomed bowl. Sprinkle in SOY LECITHIN. Using a hand blender, blend for 3 to 4 minutes, then let sit for 5 minutes.

04   To serve, collect foam using a spoon. If needed and to obtain more foam, repeat step 3.

ASSEMBLY

05   To serve, arrange tartare and foam on plates, then decorate each plate with one caperberry and a few edible flower petals.

Sa Cl 🍬🥄 Aa ✏️ Aa 🧴🔌

DECADENT DECONSTRUCTION

DIFFICULTY   3/5
ACTIVE TIME   0:30
TOTAL TIME   1:30
*TIPS ON PEARLS   P. 22
*TIPS ON SPHERES   P. 46
*TIPS ON SPAGHETTIS   P. 24

INGREDIENTS

tall glass of oil

MATCHA-PISTACHIO BUTTER

2 tbs (30 ml) unsalted butter
1 tbs (15 ml) icing sugar
1 tsp (5 ml) matcha tea powder
a dash lemon juice
2 tsp (10 ml) ground pistachios

COCONUT MILK SPHERES

¾ cup (190 ml) coconut milk
2 tbs (30 ml) sugar
½ tsp (2.5 ml) CALCIUM LACTATE
1 sachet (2 g) SODIUM ALGINATE

MANDARIN JUICE PEARLS

1 tbs (15 ml) honey
6 mandarins
1 sachet (2 g) AGAR-AGAR

BLACKBERRY JUICE SPAGHETTIS

3 cups (750 ml) blackberries
2 tbs (30 ml) honey
4 cups (1 l) ice cubes
1 sachet (2 g) AGAR-AGAR

TO SERVE

mâche
olive oil
lemon juice
edible flowers

DIRECTIONS

MATCHA-PISTACHIO BUTTER

01 Soften butter in a pan or microwave. In a bowl, combine icing sugar and matcha. Incorporate butter and lemon juice and mix well, then add in pistachios and mix some more until homogenous. Place on a sheet of parchment paper and refrigerate.

COCONUT MILK SPHERES*

02 Combine coconut milk and sugar, then mix in CALCIUM LACTATE until is completely dissolved. Pour mixture into small, demi-spherical molds and let sit in the freezer, along with the glass of oil, for 1 hour or until the spheres are frozen (while you wait, make MANDARIN JUICE PEARLS and BLACKBERRY JUICE SPAGHETTIS).

03 In a rectangular, flat-bottomed bowl and using a hand blender, dissolve SODIUM ALGINATE in 2 cups water. Let sit for 15 minutes.

04 Unmold frozen spheres in alginate bath. Let sit for 3 minutes while gently stirring once in a while to prevent the spheres from touching.

05 Fill a medium-sized bowl with water. Using a slotted spoon, delicately collect the spheres and briefly rinse them in the water, then remove excess water from each sphere by applying a piece of paper towel on the bottom of the spoon. Reserve.

MANDARIN JUICE PEARLS*

06 Using a juicer, extract juice from mandarins. Filter 1 cup of the juice, then reduce to 3/4 of a cup on medium heat. Incorporate honey and AGAR-AGAR. Bring to a boil, then remove from heat immediately.

07 Remove oil from freezer or refrigerator. Using a pipette held at a 90° angle, slowly drip droplets of the agar-agar preparation in the cold oil. Pour onto a sieve and above the sink to get rid of the oil and rinse under cold water. Set aside.

BLACKBERRY JUICE SPAGHETTIS*

08 Place ice cubes in a large bowl and fill with cold water.

09 Using a juicer, extract juice from blackberries. Filter ¾ of a cup (190 ml) of the juice. In a pot, combine with honey and AGAR-AGAR. Bring to a boil, then remove from heat immediately.

10 Fill a food grade syringe with the agar-agar preparation. Plug syringe into a silicone tube and fill up the tube, then place it in the ice bath for 1 minute. Remove the tube from the ice bath, then, using the syringe again, push air into the tube to eject the spaghetti. Repeat until enough spaghettis are obtained.

ASSEMBLY

11 First, assemble a salad of mâche, olive oil and lemon juice on each plate, topped with a few edible flowers. Then, arrange matcha-pistachio butter, coconut milk spheres, mandarin juice pearls and blackberry juice spaghetti on each plate as pictured.

MODERNIZED TAGLIATELLE

DIFFICULTY   2/5
ACTIVE TIME   0:30
TOTAL TIME   1:30
*TIPS ON PEARLS   P. 22

INGREDIENTS

2 tall glasses filled with oil

HONEY PEARLS

¾ cup (190 ml) honey
¼ cup (65 ml) water
1 sachet (2 g) AGAR-AGAR

BALSAMIC VINEGAR PEARLS

1 cup (250 ml) balsamic vinegar
1 sachet (2 g) AGAR-AGAR

PARMESAN BROCCOLI PUREE

3 cups (750 ml) broccoli florets
¾ cup (190 ml) grated parmesan
¼ cup (65 ml) butter
¼ cup (65 ml) heavy cream
salt and pepper, to taste

LEMON BUTTER

½ cup (125 ml) butter
juice of ½ a lemon
pepper, to taste

TO SERVE

cooked tagliatelle
extra parmesan

DIRECTIONS

01 Refrigerate both glasses of oil to cool overnight, or, to save time, place them in the freezer for 1 hour before starting.

HONEY PEARLS*

02 In a pot, bring honey and water to a boil with 1 sachet of AGAR-AGAR, then remove from heat immediately.

03 Remove 1 glass of oil from the freezer or refrigerator. Using a pipette held at a 90° angle, slowly drip droplets of the agar-agar preparation in the cold oil. Pour onto a sieve and above the sink to get rid of the oil and rinse under cold water. Set aside.

BALSAMIC VINEGAR PEARLS*

04 In a pot, bring balsamic vinegar to a boil with 1 sachet of AGAR-AGAR, then remove from heat immediately.

05 Remove remaining glass of oil from the freezer or refrigerator. Using a pipette held at a 90° angle, slowly drip droplets of the agar-agar preparation in the cold oil. Pour onto a sieve and above the sink to get rid of the oil and rinse under cold water. Set aside.

PARMESAN BROCCOLI PUREE

06 Steam broccoli until tender, then puree in a food processor. Season and mix in parmesan. Add in cream to taste. Serve warm, using a pastry bag.

LEMON BUTTER

07 Warm butter on low heat until it simmers. Mix in lemon juice and let simmer for 1 more minute. Serve immediately.

ASSEMBLY

08 Coat pasta in lemon butter and divide between serving spoons. Top with pearls and parmesan broccoli puree. Add parmesan to taste.

HAM-WRAPPED MELON SUSHI

DIFFICULTY	3/5
ACTIVE TIME	0:30
TOTAL TIME	0:30
*TIPS ON CAVIAR	P. 42

INGREDIENTS

MELON CAVIAR

1 cantaloupe melon
1 tbs (15 g) sugar
2 cups (500 ml) water
1 sachet (2 g) SODIUM ALGINATE
1 sachet (5 g) CALCIUM LACTATE

TO SERVE

6 croutons
6 slices prosciutto
2 tbs (30 ml) olive oil
orange zest
pepper
olive oil

DIRECTIONS

MELON CAVIAR*

01 Peel the melon and cut it into cubes. Process the cubes of cantaloupe in a blender until a uniform texture is obtained and strain the contents through a sieve.

02 In a rectangular, flat-bottomed bowl and using a hand blender, dissolve 1 sachet of SODIUM ALGINATE in 1 cup (250 ml) of the cantaloupe coulis made in the previous step and sugar. Let sit for 10 minutes.

03 Dissolve 1 sachet of CALCIUM LACTATE in 2 cups (500 ml) of water using a spoon. Then, using a pipette held at a 90° angle, slowly drip droplets of the alginate solution into the calcium lactate bath. Let sit for 3 minutes, then empty the calcium lactate bath into the sink and onto a sieve so you're left with just the melon caviar. Rinse in lukewarm water.

ASSEMBLY

04 Wrap a slice of prosciutto around a crouton to create a bowl shape. Fill with the melon caviar, garnish with the zest and pepper and drizzle with olive oil.

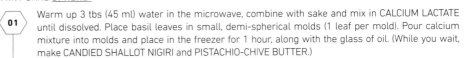

VEGETARIAN
NIGIRI PLATTER

DIFFICULTY   3/5
ACTIVE TIME   1:15
TOTAL TIME   1:15
*TIPS ON PEARLS   P. 22
*TIPS ON SPHERES   P. 46
*TIPS ON FOAM   P. 56

INGREDIENTS

1 tall glass filled with oil

MINT SAKE SPHERE

4 fl oz (120 ml) sake
3 tbs (45 ml) oz water
10 small mint leaves
2 cups (500 ml) water
½ tsp (2.5 ml) CALCIUM LACTATE
1 sachet (2 g) SODIUM ALGINATE

CANDIED SHALLOT SUSHI

2 cups (500ml) sliced shallots
2 tbs (30 ml) olive oil
2 tbs (30 ml) butter
2 tbs (30 ml) maple syrup
¾ cup (190 ml) white wine
¼ cup (65 ml) wine vinegar
1 bay leaf
water
salt and pepper, to taste

PISTACHIO-CHIVE BUTTER

½ cup (125 ml) skinless pistachios
1 tsp (5 ml) grapeseed oil
½ bunch chives
½ tsp (2.5 ml) lime juice
salt, to taste

PASSIONFRUIT PEARLS

2 cups (500 ml) passionfruit juice
a pinch saffron
1 sachet (2 g) AGAR-AGAR

SOY SAUCE FOAM

1 cup (250 ml) soy sauce
½ cup (125 ml) water
1 sachet (2 g) SOY LECITHIN

TO SERVE

2 cups (500 ml) cooked sushi rice
shiso leaves

DIRECTIONS

MINT SAKE SPHERE*

01 Warm up 3 tbs (45 ml) water in the microwave, combine with sake and mix in CALCIUM LACTATE until dissolved. Place basil leaves in small, demi-spherical molds (1 leaf per mold). Pour calcium mixture into molds and place in the freezer for 1 hour, along with the glass of oil. (While you wait, make CANDIED SHALLOT NIGIRI and PISTACHIO-CHIVE BUTTER.)

02 In a rectangular, flat-bottomed bowl, use a hand blender to dissolve 1 sachet SODIUM ALGINATE in 2 cups (500 ml) of water. Warm up in the microwave.

03 Unmold frozen spheres in alginate bath. Let sit for 3 minutes while gently stirring once in a while to prevent the spheres from touching.

04 Fill a medium-sized bowl with water. Using a slotted spoon, delicately collect the spheres and briefly rinse them in the water, then remove excess water from each sphere by applying a piece of paper towel on the bottom of the spoon. Reserve.

CANDIED SHALLOT NIGIRI

05 Reduce wine vinegar on low heat for 10 minutes, until syrupy. While you wait, peel shallots (be careful to leave them whole).

06 In a large pan, heat butter and oil. Arrange the shallots in the pan without piling them up, add salt and bay leaf, and cook without turning for 5 minutes. Then, add in syrup and about 4 tbs (60 ml) reduced vinegar and heat through. Pour in water (the shallots should be sitting in it but not covered by it) and cover with a sheet of wax paper. Cook for 10 minutes.

07 Remove wax paper, wet with wine, and cook for about 30 minutes, stirring delicately once in a while to coat onions. Add in more wine if the liquid reduces too much. (While you wait, make PISTACHIO-CHIVE BUTTER.) By the end, the onions should appear caramelized and glossy.

PISTACHIO-CHIVE BUTTER

08 Preheat oven to 300°F (175°C) and finely chop chives. Roast pistachios in oven for 10 minutes.

08 In a food processor, pulse roasted pistachios into a fine powder. Continue blending as you gradually add in oil. Transfer to a bowl and mix in lime juice, chives and salt. Reserve.

PASSIONFRUIT PEARLS*

09 Reduce juice to 1 cup (250 ml). Bring to a boil with saffron and AGAR-AGAR, then remove from heat immediately.

10 Remove oil from freezer. Using a pipette held at a 90° angle, slowly drip droplets of the agar-agar preparation in the cold oil. Pour onto a sieve and above the sink to get rid of the oil and rinse under cold water. Set aside.

SOY SAUCE FOAM*

11 In a rectangular, flat-bottomed bowl, combine water and soy sauce and sprinkle in SOY LECITHIN. Using a hand blender, blend for 3 to 4 minutes, then let sit for 5 minutes.

12 To serve, collect foam using a spoon. If needed and to obtain more foam, repeat step 11.

ASSEMBLY

13 Halve candied shallots and roll rice into balls. Brush each rice ball with a bit of pistachio-chive butter and top with half a shallot. Serve on plates with a shiso leaf, a sake sphere, a few passionfruit pearls, a big spoonful of balsamic emulsion, and some more pistachio butter.

DECONSTRUCTED PLATTER

DIFFICULTY	3/5
ACTIVE TIME	1:15
TOTAL TIME	2:15
*TIPS ON PEARLS	P. 22
*TIPS ON FOAM	P. 56

INGREDIENTS

tall glass of oil
4 sea urchins

CREAM OF ROASTED CAULIFLOWER

2 tbs (30 ml) olive oil
½ tsp (2.5 ml) cumin
2 tsp (10 ml) smoked paprika
1 tsp (5 ml) sea salt
a pinch Espelette pepper
1 head cauliflower
2 tbs (30 ml) butter
1 onion
2 garlic cloves
sea salt, to taste
pepper, to taste
1 tsp (5 ml) thyme leaves
2 cups (500 ml) chicken stock
½ cup (125 ml) heavy cream
juice of 4 urchins

SQUID INK PEARLS

¾ cup (190 ml) squid ink
1 sachet (2 g) AGAR-AGAR

ANISEED FOAM

1 ½ cups (375 ml) aniseed liqueur
1 sachet (2 g) SOY LECITHIN

TO SERVE

4 urchins' tongues
½ of an apple
fennel shoots
mâche
as dash lemon juice
a drizzle olive oil

DIRECTIONS

 01 First, place oil in the refrigerator to cool overnight, or, to save time, place it in the freezer for 1 hour.

 02 Open up urchins on the flat side by cutting into the shell with scissors. Remove, rinse and reserve the orange parts (also called urchin tongues). Also reserve juices. Remove the urchins' spikes and reserve as well.

CREAM OF ROASTED CAULIFLOWER

 03 Preheat oven to 425 °F (220 °C). Cut cauliflower into florets and chop onion and garlic.

 04 In a bowl, combine oil, cumin, paprika, sea salt and Espelette pepper. Mix in cauliflower florets and transfer to a baking sheet. Cook for 25-30 minutes, tossing often. While you wait, soften onion in butter, in a large pot, until translucent. Mix in garlic and season.

 05 Mix in roasted cauliflower, thyme and chicken stock and bring to a boil. Simmer for 5 minutes, then pour in cream and urchin juices. Turn off heat and use a hand blender to blend until homogenous and smooth.

SQUID INK **PEARLS***

 06 Bring squid ink to a boil with AGAR-AGAR, then remove from heat immediately.

07 Remove oil from freezer or refrigerator. Using a pipette held at a 90° angle, slowly drip droplets of the agar-agar preparation in the cold oil. Pour onto a sieve and above the sink to get rid of the oil and rinse under cold water. Set aside.

ANISEED **FOAM***

08 Pour aniseed liqueur into a rectangular, flat-bottomed bowl. Sprinkle in SOY LECITHIN. Using a hand blender, blend for 3 to 4 minutes, then let sit for 5 minutes.

09 To serve, collect foam using a spoon. If needed and to obtain more foam, repeat step 8.

ASSEMBLY

10 Cut apple into a small dice. To serve, fill sea urchin shells with hot cream of cauliflower. Top with urchin tongues, apple dice and aniseed foam. Decorate each plate as pictured with shoots, mâche and squid ink pearls. Finish with a dash of lemon juice and a drizzle of olive oil.

VIOLET SEA

INGREDIENTS

VIOLET WATER PEARLS

1 tall glass filled with oil
75 violet flowers
juice of 1 lemon
½ cup (125 ml) sugar
¾ cup (190 ml) water
1 sachet (2 g) AGAR-AGAR

BLUE POTATO SPHERES

2-4 blue potatoes
salt to taste

SPICY HAZELNUT-CRUSTED JOHN DORY

2 tbs (30 ml) honey
2 tbs (30 ml) tamari
1 tbs (15 ml) lime juice
1 clove garlic
2 tbs (30 ml) toasted sesame oil
4 skinless John Dory filets
1 cup (250 ml) dry-roasted hazelnuts
½ cup (125 ml) panko
1 tsp (5 ml) Espelette pepper
1 tsp (5 ml) Korean pepper flakes
salt to taste
pepper to taste

BABY BOK CHOY

2 baby bok choy bulbs
1 tbs (15 ml) butter
2 tbs chicken broth

ARTICHOKE CREAM

9 oz (270 g) frozen artichoke hearts
1 cup (250 ml) half and half
1 clove garlic
⅛ tsp (a pinch) Espelette pepper
2 tsp (10 ml) lemon juice
salt to taste

DIRECTIONS

 01 Rinse flowers in cold water and place them in a bowl with the lemon juice. Crush without mashing, then let sit overnight. Refrigerate tall glass of oil until very cold, or, to save time, place it in the freezer for 1 hour before using. Lastly, let artichokes thaw overnight in the refrigerator.

VIOLET WATER PEARLS*

 02 Using a sieve placed on top of a pot, filter flower preparation and save juices. Make sure to squeeze the flowers to collect as much liquid as possible, then discard the flowers. Pour in sugar and cook on very low heat for 7 minutes.

 03 Sprinkle 1 sachet AGAR-AGAR into the pot and mix it in using a spoon. Bring to a boil, then remove from heat immediately.

 04 Remove the cold oil from the freezer or refrigerator. Using a pipette held at a 90° angle, slowly drip droplets of the agar-agar preparation into the cold oil. Stir gently, then, using a sieve, collect pearls and briefly rinse them under water. Reserve.

BLUE POTATO SPHERES

 05 Preheat oven to 350 °F (175 °C) and lightly grease a baking sheet. Wash potatoes but do not peel them, then, halve each potato (cut larger potatoes into quarters). Place potato chunks on the baking sheet and sprinkle with salt, then cook in the oven for 35 minutes. (While the potatoes are cooking, start making SPICY HAZELNUT-CRUSTED JOHN DORY).

 06 Once the potatoes are done cooking, use an ice cream scoop to scoop spheres out of the flesh. Reserve spheres in a bowl covered with a damp cloth to prevent them from drying or getting cold.

SPICY HAZELNUT-CRUSTED JOHN DORY

 07 Line a baking sheet with parchment paper. Mince garlic, then whisk it together with honey, tamari, lime juice, and sesame oil. Using a pastry brush, generously coat filets with the mixture and reserve.

 08 Chop hazelnuts. In a bowl, mix them together with panko, Espelette pepper, Korean pepper flakes, salt and pepper. Transfer onto a large cutting board, then roll coated filets in crust mix until the surface is homogenously covered in it.

 09 Once the potatoes are out of the oven, turn it up to 425 °F (220 °C). (While the oven is heating up, make BABY BOK CHOY.) Once the oven has reached the desired temperature, place filets on baking sheet and cook for 13-15 minutes. (While the filets are cooking, make ARTICHOKE CREAM.)

BABY BOK CHOY

 10 Slice bulbs lengthwise and cook with butter in a pan, on medium heat, for about 2 minutes. Season with salt and pepper, then add in broth and let reduce for another 2 minutes. Remove from heat, cover and reserve.

ARTICHOKE CREAM

 11 Chop artichokes coarsely and smash garlic, then combine in a pan with half and half, Espelette pepper and salt. Cover and cook on medium heat for 5 minutes. Uncover and cook for 5 more minutes, until artichokes are tender. Remove from heat and stir in lemon juice. Using a hand blender, blend until homogenous.

ASSEMBLY

 12 Divide artichoke cream, filets, baby bok choy and blue potato spheres between 4 plates. Decorate with violet water pearls, and serve.

JAPANESE SUNSET AIRS

DIFFICULTY 1/5
ACTIVE TIME 0:05
TOTAL TIME 0:05
*TIPS ON FOAM P. 56

INGREDIENTS

1 ¼ cup (315 ml) blood orange juice
2 fl oz (60 ml) sake
1 fl oz (30 ml) lychee syrup
1 sachet (2 g) SOY LECITHIN

NOTE

You can replace the freshly squeezed blood orange juice with your favorite fruit juice.

DIRECTIONS

FOAM*

01 Pour juice into a rectangular, flat-bottomed bowl and sprinkle in SOY LECITHIN. Using a hand blender, blend for 3 to 4 minutes, then let sit for 5 minutes. For different color foams, repeat with any fruit juice.

02 In a cocktail shaker, shake together sake and syrup. Pour into a glass and top with blood orange foam.

GEOMETRIC TARTARE

DIFFICULTY   2/5
ACTIVE TIME   0:30
TOTAL TIME   0:30
*TIPS ON CANNELLONIS   P. 26

INGREDIENTS

YUZU CANNELLONIS

¾ cup (190 ml) chicken stock
1 tbs (15 ml) cold butter
1 yuzu (or lemon)
1 tsp (5 ml) honey
salt, to taste
pepper, to taste
1 sachet (2 g) AGAR-AGAR

GEOMETRIC TARTARE

1 18-oz salmon filet
2 shallots
2 garlic cloves
4 tbs (60 ml) olive oil
1 tbs (15 ml) Dijon mustard
1 tbs (15 ml) Japanese mayo
1 tbs (15 ml) panko
1 tbs (15 ml) dill
1 tbs (15 ml) yuzu (or lemon) juice
1 tsp (5 ml) yuzu (or lemon) zest
2 tbs (30 ml) capers
a few drops sriracha
salt, to taste
pepper, to taste

BUTTER ASPARAGUS

1 bunch asparagus
2 tbs (30 ml) butter
salt, to taste
pepper, to taste

TO SERVE

raspberries
microgreens
black sesame seeds

DIRECTIONS

YUZU CANNELLONIS*

 01 First, zest yuzu (you will not need the actual fruit). Combine zest with all other ingredients in a pot along with AGAR-AGAR. Bring to a boil, then remove from heat immediately.

 02 Pour a small amount of the preparation onto a plate and into a thin layer. Tilt the plate as you pour to cover as much surface as possible. Refrigerate the plate and repeat. Take out of the refrigerator 10 minutes before serving so the cannellonis can warm up, and cut them into small rectangles using a knife.

GEOMETRIC TARTARE

 03 First, remove skin from filet and dice it small. Finely chop shallots, garlic, dill and capers, and blanch zest. Then, combine all ingredients in a bowl and reserve. Use a square cutter to serve as pictured.

BUTTER ASPARAGUS

 04 Cook asparagus in butter on medium heat. Season, then reserve.

ASSEMBLY

 05 First, place a tartare square in the center of each plate. Wrap 3 asparagus spears in a yuzu square and place on top of a tartare square, then repeat. Decorate each plate with raspberries, microgreens and sesame seeds as pictured.

VEAL STOCK CHIPS & MAPLE FILETS

DIFFICULTY   2/5
ACTIVE TIME   1:00
TOTAL TIME   4:00

INGREDIENTS

VEAL STOCK

2 lbs (900 g) veal bones
½ gallon (2l) water
2 garlic cloves
1 onion
1 carrot
1 leek
2 celery sticks
4 tbs (60 ml) tomato paste
1 cup (250 ml) mushrooms
1 tbs (15 ml) pepper
2 bay leaves
1 tsp (5 ml) salt

VEAL STOCK CHIPS

¾ cup (190 ml) veal stock
1 sachet (2 g) AGAR-AGAR

CARAMELIZED ONIONS

4 onions
¼ cup (65 ml) olive oil
1 tbs (15 ml) maple syrup
salt and pepper, to taste

CANDIED POTATOES

2 cups (500 ml) potato bells
¼ cup (65 ml) olive oil
3 garlic cloves
2 thyme sprigs
2 rosemary sprigs
salt and pepper, to taste

MAPLE-KUMQUAT PORK

2 1-lb pork filets (450 g)
all-purpose flour
1 tbs (15 ml) butter
1 tbs (15 ml) olive oil
4 shallots
1 tbs (15 ml) Dijon mustard
½ cup (125 ml) maple syrup
⅓ cup (85 ml) kumquat or orange juice
salt and pepper, to taste
a few thyme sprigs

DIRECTIONS

VEAL STOCK

 Preheat oven to 450 °F (230 °C). Place bones on a baking sheet and roast for 10 minutes. Peel and slice onion, carrot and leek (do not use the leek's green part). Slice celery and mushrooms.

 Place bones in a large pot. Cover with water, then bring to a boil. Add in all other ingredients and let simmer on low heat for 90 minutes while skimming once in a while. When done, filter through a sieve (discard all solid ingredients) and let cool down before storing in the refrigerator.

VEAL STOCK CHIPS

 Reduce 1 cup (250 ml) of veal stock to ¾ cup (190 ml) on low heat. Bring to a boil with AGAR-AGAR, then remove from heat immediately.

 Pour a small amount of the preparation onto a plate and into a thin layer. Tilt the plate as you pour to cover as much surface as possible. Refrigerate the plate for 10 minutes and repeat.

 Take plates out of the refrigerator and cut veal stock jelly sheets into small rectangles. Dry using a dehydrator or, alternatively, turn the oven on to the lowest setting and cook for 1 hour on a baking sheet, with the oven door partially open.

CARAMELIZED ONIONS

 Preheat oven to 350 °F (175 °C). Halve onions, then combine all other ingredients in a large bowl. Coat onions with glaze, then transfer to a large baking sheet, cut side facing up. Cook for 75 minutes, turning once halfway through cooking time.

CANDIED POTATOES

 As soon as the onions are in the oven, halve potatoes and garlic, then combine with all other ingredients in a large baking dish. Put in the oven, on the same rack as the onions, and cook for the same amount of time, tossing often.

MAPLE-KUMQUAT PORK

 When there is only 30 minutes left of cooking time left for onions and potatoes, finely chop shallots. Cover filets in a thin layer of flour, then brown them with butter and oil in a pan. Remove filets from pan and cook in the oven for 16 minutes. Let sit for 5 minutes before slicing.

 While the filets are cooking, use the same pan to brown the shallots in butter. Add in mustard, maple syrup and kumquat juice and simmer for 3 minutes or until the sauce thickens. Once the filets are done cooking, cut them, put them back in the pan and toss to coat.

ASSEMBLY

 Serve the filets on plates with onions, potatoes and veal stock chips.

QUINOA FORESTIERE WITH BERRY CAPSULES

DIFFICULTY	3/5
ACTIVE TIME	1:30
TOTAL TIME	3:30
*TIPS ON PEARLS	P. 22
*TIPS ON SPHERES	P. 46
*TIPS ON FOAM	P. 56

INGREDIENTS

QUINOA

1 cup (250 ml) black quinoa
2 cups (500 ml) vegetable broth
3 rosemary sprigs
a pinch sea salt
1 tbs (15 ml) lemon juice
a dash olive oil
salt, to taste
pepper, to taste

MUSHROOMS CHIPS

10 girolles
1-2 king oyster mushrooms
8 oz (240 g) dried mushrooms
sea salt, to taste

VEGAN SHALLOT MAYO

1 cup (250 ml) cashews
¼ cup (65 ml) chopped cauliflower
½ cup (125 ml) filtered water
¼ cup (65 ml) olive oil
1 tsp (5 ml) Dijon mustard
1 tsp (5 ml) agave nectar
1 tsp (5 ml) apple cider vinegar
a pinch sea salt
2 tbs (30 ml) lemon juice
1 tbs (15 ml) chopped shallots

RAPSBERRY SPHERES

2 cups (500 ml) water
1 ⅔ cups (415 ml) raspberries
1 tsp (5 ml) sugar
1 sachet (2 g) SODIUM ALGINATE
½ tsp (2.5 ml) CALCIUM LACTATE

BLACKBERRY PEARLS

1 tall glass filled with oil
3 cups (750 ml) blackberries
2 tbs (30 ml) honey
1 sachet (2 g) AGAR-AGAR

LEMON FOAM

⅔ cup (170 ml) water
⅔ cup (170 ml) lemon juice
1 sachet (2 g) SOY LECITHIN

TO SERVE

chervil
extra blackberries

DIRECTIONS

01 Soak cashews in water for at least 2 hours or overnight. Place oil (both the tall glass and the ¼ cup (60 ml)) in the refrigerator to cool overnight, or, to save time, place it in the freezer for 1 hour.

QUINOA

02 Cook quinoa in broth with rosemary sprigs and sea salt. Follow package instructions. (While the quinoa is cooking, start making MUSHROOM CHIPS) Once done, take off heat, remove rosemary sprigs, mix in lemon juice and olive oil and season to taste, then cover and reserve.

MUSHROOM CHIPS

03 Prepare a fryer or, alternatively, fill a large pot with cooking oil and bring it to about 350 °F (175 °C). Also prepare a few plates lined with paper towels.

04 Using a blender, grind dehydrated mushrooms into a fine powder. Thinly slice king oysters and girolles, lengthwise. Place a small batch of sliced oysters and girolles in hot oil and let them brown while stirring with a skimmer. Once done, transfer to a lined plate and sprinkle with mushroom powder. Repeat until all mushrooms are fried.

VEGAN SHALLOT MAYO

05 Discard the cashew soaking water and remove ¼ cup (60 ml) cold oil from the refrigerator or freezer. In a blender, combine cashews with cauliflower while adding water in very gradually, until homogenous. Then, continue blending while gradually adding oil in, until the mixture becomes creamy. Finally, blend in all other ingredients and season to taste.

RAPSBERRY SPHERES*

06 In a rectangular, flat-bottomed bowl, use a hand blender to dissolve 1 sachet SODIUM ALGINATE in water, then refrigerate for 15 minutes. While you wait, blend raspberries and sugar together with CALCIUM LACTATE in a blender.

07 Remove cooled sodium alginate bath from the refrigerator. Using a measuring spoon, deposit spoonfuls of the calcium lactate mixture in the alginate bath and let sit for 3 minutes. Stir gently with a slotted spoon to prevent the spheres from touching one another.

08 Once done, gently remove spheres from the bath using the slotted spoon and remove any excess water by applying a piece of paper towel to the bottom of the spoon. Reserve.

BLACKBERRY PEARLS*

09 Using a juicer, extract juice from blackberries. Filter ¾ cup (190 ml) of the juice. Bring to a boil with honey and AGAR-AGAR, then remove from heat immediately.

10 Remove oil from freezer or refrigerator. Using a pipette held at a 90° angle, slowly drip droplets of the agar-agar preparation in the cold oil. Pour onto a sieve and above the sink to get rid of the oil and rinse under cold water. Set aside.

LEMON FOAM*

11 In a rectangular, flat-bottomed bowl, combine water and lemon juice and sprinkle in SOY LECITHIN. Using a hand blender, blend for 3 to 4 minutes, then let sit for 5 minutes. To serve, collect foam using a spoon. If needed and to obtain more foam, repeat step 11.

ASSEMBLY

12 Divide quinoa and lemon foam on plates decorated with chervil and blackberries. Top lemon foam with blackberry pearls and quinoa with mushroom chips and raspberry spheres. Serve with vegan mayo on the side.

ENCAPSULATED ENTREMETS

DIFFICULTY 1/5
ACTIVE TIME 0:10
TOTAL TIME 1:05
*TIPS ON SPHERES P. 46

INGREDIENTS

ALMOND LIQUEUR SPHERES

5 fl oz (150 ml) almond liqueur
2 cups (500 ml) water
½ tsp (2.5 ml) CALCIUM LACTATE
1 sachet (2 g) SODIUM ALGINATE

LEMON ICE SHAVINGS

water
lemon juice

TO SERVE

a few lemon ice shavings
cubed pitaya

DIRECTIONS

ALMOND LIQUEUR **SPHERES***

01 Warm up 1 tbs (15 ml) of water and combine with CALCIUM LACTATE. Stir until the calcium lactate is fully diluted, then combine with liqueur and pour mixture into small, demi-spherical molds and let sit in the freezer for 1 hour or until the spheres are frozen. (While you wait, make LEMON ICE SHAVINGS.)

02 In a rectangular, flat-bottomed bowl and using a hand blender, dissolve SODIUM ALGINATE in remaining water. Let sit for 15 minutes, then warm briefly in a microwave oven.

03 Unmold frozen liqueur spheres in alginate bath. Let sit for 3 minutes while gently stirring once in a while to prevent the spheres from touching.

04 Fill a medium-sized bowl with water. Using a slotted spoon, delicately collect the spheres and briefly rinse them in the water, then remove excess water from each sphere by applying a piece of paper towel on the bottom of the spoon. Reserve.

LEMON ICE SHAVINGS

05 Combine 2 parts water and 1 part lemon juice and pour onto a shallow plate, then place in the freezer for 1 hour. Take out of the freezer just before serving and crack into small pieces.

ASSEMBLY

06 To serve, dress plates with a thin layer of lemon ice shavings, add a pitaya cube, and top with an almond liqueur sphere.

RARE
RISOTTO

DIFFICULTY   3/5
ACTIVE TIME   1:15
TOTAL TIME   2:00

INGREDIENTS

RARE STEAK

20 oz (600 g) flap steak
½ cup (125 ml) olive oil
2 tbs (30 ml) lemon juice
1 garlic clove
1 tbs (15 ml) honey
1 tbs (15 ml) parsley
2 tbs (30 ml) chives
salt, to taste
pepper, to taste
1 tbs (15 ml) butter

BLACKCURRANT CHIPS

1 cup (250 ml) blackcurrant syrup
1 sachet (2 g) AGAR-AGAR

RISOTTO

5 cups beef stock
½ cup (125 ml) dried mushrooms
1 cup (250 ml) white mushrooms
3 cups (750 ml) wild mushrooms
1 onion
2 garlic cloves
2 cups (500 ml) arborio rice
1 cup (250 ml) white wine
½ cup (125 ml) grated parmesan
2 tbs (30 ml) butter
a drizzle olive oil
salt, to taste
pepper, to taste

TO SERVE

edible flowers
sautéed girolles
pickled garlic cloves

DIRECTIONS

RARE STEAK

01 First, cut flap steak into four. Finely chop garlic, parsley and chives.

02 Combine all ingredients, except for the steaks and butter, in a resealable plastic bag, and shake. Add in steaks and marinate for 2 hours in the refrigerator. (While you wait, make the BLACKCURRANT CHIPS and RISOTTO.)

03 Warm butter in a pan on medium-high heat. Cook each steak for 2 minutes on each side, then let sit for 2 minutes on a cutting board before serving.

BLACKCURRANT CHIPS

04 Reduce syrup to ¾ cup (190 ml) on low heat. Bring to a boil with AGAR-AGAR, then remove from heat immediately.

05 Pour a small amount of the preparation onto a plate and into a thin layer. Tilt the plate as you pour to cover as much surface as possible. Refrigerate the plate for 10 minutes and repeat.

06 Take plates out of the refrigerator and cut blackcurrant jelly sheets into small rectangles. Dry using a dehydrator or, alternatively, turn the oven on to the lowest setting and cook for 1 hour on a baking sheet, with the oven door partially open. (while you wait, make RISOTTO.)

RISOTTO

07 First, coarsely chop dried mushrooms, slice fresh mushrooms, and chop onion and garlic. Bring beef stock to a boil with dried mushrooms, then bring down to a simmer just to keep it all warm.

08 In a large pot, sauté fresh mushrooms in oil. Season generously, then reserve in a bowl. In the same large pot (now empty), brown onion in oil. Add in garlic and cook for 1 more minute. Stir in rice, add in white wine and reduce until the rice has absorbed all liquid. Gradually add in mushroom broth, waiting long enough between each ladleful for the rice to absorb the liquid. Add in parmesan, sautéed mushrooms and butter with the last ladleful. Mix well.

ASSEMBLY

09 First, slice steaks into strips. Divide risotto between plates and top with meat. Decorate each plate with blackcurrant chips, edible flowers, girolles, almonds and garlic.

VEGETARIAN RISOTTO & PEARLS

DIFFICULTY	2/5
ACTIVE TIME	0:45
TOTAL TIME	1:45
*TIPS ON PEARLS	P. 22

INGREDIENTS

BUTTERNUT PUREE

½ onion
1 glove garlic
1 butternut squash
1 tbs (15 ml) butter
½ cup (125 ml) vegetable broth

QUINOA RISOTTO

1 cup (250 ml) quinoa, rinsed
2 onions
butternut puree
3 cups (750 ml) vegetable broth
½ cup (125 ml) dry-roasted hazelnuts
¼ cup (65 ml) dry-roasted cashews
1 tbs (15 ml) butter
6 leaves Savoy cabbage
sea salt, to taste
pepper, to taste

RED WINE SAUCE

1 cup (250 ml) red wine
¼ cup (65 ml) shallots, finely chopped
¼ cup (65 ml) vegetarian demi-glace sauce
3 thyme sprigs
1 bay leaf
1 rosemary sprig
2 tbs (30 ml) unsalted butter

PEPPERY LEMON PEARLS

1 tall glass oil
1 cup (250 ml) lemon juice
1 tbs (15 ml) cane sugar
pepper, to taste
1 sachet (2 g) AGAR-AGAR

TO SERVE

microgreens
edible flower petals
capers

DIRECTIONS

 01 Refrigerate the tall glass filled with oil to cool overnight, or, to save time, place it in the freezer for 1 hour.

BUTTERNUT PUREE

 02 First, chop garlic (finely) and onion and dice squash. Then, in a pot, heat up butter and soften the onion and garlic. Add in squash and cook for 5 more minutes. Add in broth and let simmer for 20 minutes. (While you wait, start making QUINOA RISOTTO.) Puree in a food processor, season, and reserve.

QUINOA RISOTTO

 03 Chop onion, cashews and hazelnuts and blanch cabbage. Brown onion in butter for 4 minutes. Season, then mix in quinoa. Gradually add in broth over 15-20 minutes while stirring often and giving it time to reduce between each ladleful. Halfway through cooking time, add in the nuts. Once risotto is cooked, stir in butternut puree.

04 Divide risotto between cabbage leaves and close them to form papillotes. 10 minutes before serving, warm the papillotes on low heat.

WINE SAUCE

 05 Chop shallots. Then, in a small pot, combine them with wine and demi-glace sauce. Add thyme sprigs, bay leaves and rosemary sprigs and bring to a boil, then let simmer until liquid has reduced by half.

06 Use a sieve to filter the liquid (discard solid ingredients), then put it back in the pot. Add in butter and cook, stirring constantly, until smooth and homogenous. Season.

PEPPERY LEMON **PEARLS***

 07 In a pot, reduce lemon juice to ¾ of a cup (190 ml). Add in AGAR-AGAR, sugar and a generous dose of pepper. Bring to a boil, then remove from heat immediately.

 08 Remove oil from the freezer or refrigerator. Using a pipette held at a 90° angle, slowly drip droplets of the agar-agar preparation in the cold oil. Pour onto a sieve and above the sink to get rid of the oil and rinse under cold water. Set aside.

ASSEMBLY

 09 First, mix lemon pearls into wine sauce and pour this mixture onto plates. Place a risotto papillote on each plate and decorate with microgreens, capers and petals, then serve.

NON-TRADITIONAL THANKSGIVING

INGREDIENTS

tall glass of oil

CRANBERRY FOAM

2 cups (500 ml) pure cranberry juice
1 sachet (2 g) SOY LECITHIN

CHICKEN SUPREMES

4 boneless, skinless chicken supremes
leaves of 3 thyme sprigs
2 tbs (30 ml) olive oil
1 tbs (15 ml) butter
2 cored, diced apples
1 diced onion
½ cup (125 ml) cranberries
½ cup (125 ml) apple cider
salt and pepper, to taste

CRANBERRY PEARLS

2 ½ cups (620 ml) pure cranberry juice
1 sachet (2 g) AGAR-AGAR

SAGE CREAM

2 tbs (30 ml) butter
2 shallots, minced
¼ cup (65 ml) white wine
½ cup (125 ml) grated old cheddar
2 tbs (30 ml) chopped sage
leaves of 1 rosemary sprig
salt an pepper, to taste
1 cup (250 ml) heavy cream

TO SERVE

2 thick slices rustic bread
dried cranberries
orange supremes
candied oranges
rosemary sprigs

DIRECTIONS

01 Refrigerate oil to cool overnight, or, to save time, place it in the freezer for 1 hour.

CRANBERRY FOAM*

02 Reduce juice to 1 cup (250 ml) and cool in the refrigerator (While you wait, make CHICKEN SUPREMES).

03 Transfer reduced juice to a rectangular, flat-bottomed bowl. Sprinkle in SOY LECITHIN. Using a hand blender, blend for 3 to 4 minutes, then let sit for 5 minutes. Repeat this step to obtain more foam.

CHICKEN SUPREMES

04 Sprinkle chicken supremes with thyme, salt and pepper. In a large pan, heat half of the oil and butter on medium-high heat. Add in chicken supremes and cook for 3 minutes on each side, until lightly browned. Reserve on a plate.

05 Add the remaining oil and butter to the pan, along with apples, cranberries and onion. Cook, while stirring, for about 4 minutes. Add in cider, deglaze and bring to a boil. Put the chicken breasts back into the pan and cook on medium-low heat for 7 minutes or until the chicken is no longer pink on the inside (turn halfway through cooking time). Place chicken on a serving plate and cover with tin foil. Reserve apple and cranberry compote as well.

CRANBERRY PEARLS*

06 In a pot, reduce juice to 1 cup. Add in AGAR-AGAR and bring to a boil, then remove from heat immediately.

07 Remove oil from the freezer or refrigerator. Using a pipette held at a 90° angle, slowly drip droplets of the agar-agar preparation in the cold oil. Pour onto a sieve and above the sink to get rid of the oil and rinse under cold water. Set aside.

SAGE CREAM

08 Melt butter in a large pan and sauté shallots in it. Deglaze with wine and reduce for 2 to 3 minutes. Stir in cream and cheese and add in sage and rosemary as well. Season and serve immediately.

ASSEMBLY

09 First, cut bread into croutons. Place a generous spoonful of compote in the center of each plate. Top with a chicken breast and cranberry pearls. Garnish each plate with a few spoonfuls of cranberry espuma and croutons dipped in sage cream. Finish with candied orange peels, dried cranberries, an orange supreme and a rosemary sprig.

SCALLOPS & POWDERIZED LIME

INGREDIENTS

RED ONION MARINADE

1 large red onion
½ cup (125 ml) olive oil
¼ cup (65 ml) white wine vinegar
1 tbs (15 ml) Dijon mustard
½ garlic clove
½ tsp (2.5 ml) onion powder
1 tsp (5 ml) parsley
salt and pepper, to taste

BUTTER-LIME POWDER

2 tsp (10 ml) melted butter
1 tbs (15 ml) lime juice
TAPIOCA MALTODEXTRIN

SAUTÉED VEGETABLES

1 yellow beet
a few cherry tomatoes
a few mini zucchinis
2 tbs (30 ml) olive oil

SAUTÉED SCALLOPS

9 large scallops
1 tbs (15 ml) olive oil
1 tbs (15 ml) butter
salt and pepper, to taste

TO SERVE

a few blackberries
a few broad beans
lime slices

DIRECTIONS

RED ONION MARINADE

 01 Slice red onion and chop garlic and parsley finely. Combine all ingredients, then transfer to a resealable plastic bag. Add in onions and shake to coat. Refrigerate for 1 hour. (While you wait, make BUTTER-LIME POWDER, SAUTÉED VEGETABLES and SAUTÉED SCALLOPS.)

BUTTER-LIME POWDER

 02 Whisk together lime juice and butter, then gradually add in TAPIOCA MALTODEXTRIN while stirring until powdery and dry.

SAUTÉED VEGETABLES

 03 First, peel and boil yellow beet. Stem tomatoes and halve zucchinis lengthwise.

 04 Slice the boiled beet. In a large pan, sauté all vegetables with oil. Remove from heat, cover with tin foil and reserve.

SAUTÉED SCALLOPS

 05 In a pan, melt butter in olive oil on medium heat. Season scallops with salt and pepper, then cook on medium-high heat for 2 minutes on each side.

ASSEMBLY

 06 Decorate plates with blackberries, broad beans and lime slices. Sprinkle with butter-lime powder as pictured. Place scallops on top of powder and arrange sautéed vegetables around them.

DECONSTRUCTED TACO

DIFFICULTY 3/5
ACTIVE TIME 0:30
TOTAL TIME 2:00
*TIPS ON PEARLS P. 22
*TIPS ON CANNELLONIS P. 26

INGREDIENTS

tall glass of oil

LIME & CILANTRO CANNELLONIS

1 cup (250 ml) lime juice
a few cilantro leaves
1 sachet (2 g) AGAR-AGAR

HOT SAUCE TOMATO PEARLS

¾ cup (190 ml) tomato juice
2 tbs (30 ml) lime juice
1 tsp (5 ml) honey
½ tsp (2.5 ml) pepper
a pinch salt
½ tsp (2.5 ml) Tabasco
½ tsp (2.5 ml) Worcestershire sauce
½ tsp (2.5 ml) ground coriander
1 sachet (2 g) AGAR-AGAR

BEEF FILLING

14 oz (420 g) beef
1 tbs (15 ml) chili powder
¼ tsp (1.25 ml) garlic powder
¼ tsp (1.25 ml) onion powder
¼ tsp (1.25 ml) pepper flakes
¼ tsp (1.25 ml) dried oregano
½ tsp (2.5 ml) paprika
1 ½ tsp (7.5 ml) ground cumin
1 tsp (5 ml) salt
1 tsp (5 ml) pepper
2 tbs (30 ml) olive oil
1 small onion

TO SERVE

1 cup (250 ml) corn kernels
1 avocado
fresh cilantro
a few romaine leaves
1 sliced jalapeno

DIRECTIONS

01 First, refrigerate tall glass of oil overnight, or, to save time, place it in the freezer for 1 hour.

LIME & CILANTRO CANNELLONIS*

02 Finely chop cilantro. Combine with lime juice in a pot and reduce to ¾ cup (190 ml) on low heat. Bring to a boil with AGAR-AGAR, then remove from heat immediately.

03 Pour a small amount of the preparation onto a plate and into a thin layer. Tilt the plate as you pour to cover as much surface as possible. Refrigerate the plate for 10 minutes and repeat.

04 Take plates out of the refrigerator and cut jelly sheets using a round cutter. Dry using a dehydrator or, alternatively, turn the oven on to the lowest setting and cook for 1 hour on a baking sheet, with the oven door partially open. (While you wait, make BEEF FILLING and HOT SAUCE TOMATO PEARLS.)

BEEF FILLING

05 First, slice or shred beef. Combine all other ingredients, except for the oil and onion, to make taco seasoning. Combine beef and seasoning in a large, resealable plastic bag and marinate for 30 minutes in the refrigerator. (While you wait, make HOT SAUCE TOMATO PEARLS.)

06 Chop the onion. In a pan, sauté it in oil for 2 minutes. Season, then add in the beef and cook for 3 to 4 minutes.

HOT SAUCE TOMATO PEARLS*

07 Bring all ingredients to a boil together with AGAR-AGAR, then remove from heat immediately.

08 Remove oil from the freezer or refrigerator. Using a pipette held at a 90° angle, slowly drip droplets of the agar-agar preparation in the cold oil. Pour onto a sieve and above the sink to get rid of the oil and rinse under cold water. Set aside.

ASSEMBLY

09 Dice avocado and cut up romaine leaves into small pieces. Place a lime and cilantro cannelloni on a plate. Garnish each taco with grilled beef, corn, cubed avocado, cilantro leaves, romaine and hot sauce tomato pearls, and cover with a second cannelloni. Decorate each plate with sliced jalapenos.

CAESAR
BUBBLE

DIFFICULTY 3/5
ACTIVE TIME 0:15
TOTAL TIME 1:00
*TIPS ON SPHERES P. 46

INGREDIENTS

BLOODY CAESAR SPHERES

4 fl oz (120 ml) clamato juice
1 ½ fl oz (45 ml) vodka
1 tsp (5 ml) Worcestershire sauce
a few drops of red Tabasco sauce
a few cracks of black pepper
½ tsp (2.5 ml) CALCIUM LACTATE
1 sachet (2 g) SODIUM ALGINATE

TO GARNISH

key lime halves, cut width-wise
celery salt
celery leaves

DIRECTIONS

BLOODY CAESAR **SPHERES***

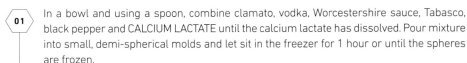

01 In a bowl and using a spoon, combine clamato, vodka, Worcestershire sauce, Tabasco, black pepper and CALCIUM LACTATE until the calcium lactate has dissolved. Pour mixture into small, demi-spherical molds and let sit in the freezer for 1 hour or until the spheres are frozen.

02 In a rectangular, flat-bottomed bowl and using a hand blender, dissolve SODIUM ALGINATE in water. Let sit for 15 minutes.

03 Unmold frozen Bloody Caesar spheres in alginate bath. Let sit for 3 minutes while gently stirring once in a while to prevent the spheres from touching.

04 Fill a medium-sized bowl with water. Using a slotted spoon, delicately collect the spheres and briefly rinse them in the water, then remove excess water from each sphere by applying a piece of paper towel on the bottom of the spoon. Reserve.

ASSEMBLY

05 With a small spoon, dig a bit into each lime half so the flesh is slightly curved inward. Place a sphere on each lime half, top with celery leaf and celery salt, and serve.

REINVENTED
GREEK SALAD

DIFFICULTY   3/5
ACTIVE TIME   0:30
TOTAL TIME   1:30
*TIPS ON SPHERES   P. 46

INGREDIENTS

SALAD

½ cup (125 ml) radishes
¾ cup (190 ml) cucumbers
1 tbs (15 ml) parsley
1 tbs (15 ml) dill

YOGURT SPHERES

1 cup (250 ml) plain yogurt
salt and pepper, to taste
1 garlic clove
2 tbs (30 ml) lemon juice
2 cups (500 ml) water
½ tsp (2.5 ml) **CALCIUM LACTATE**
1 sachet (2 g) **SODIUM ALGINATE**

TO SERVE

shiso leaves
pistachios
raspberries

DIRECTIONS

SALAD

01 Julienne radishes and cucumbers, chop parsley and dill, and combine in a bowl. Set aside.

YOGURT **SPHERES***

02 Finely chop garlic. Combine all ingredients in a bowl, except for water. Warm up 1 tbs (15 ml) of water and combine with CALCIUM LACTATE. Stir until the calcium lactate is fully diluted, then incorporate to the yogurt mixture. Pour mixture into small, demi-spherical molds and let sit in the freezer for 1 hour or until the spheres are frozen.

03 In a rectangular, flat-bottomed bowl and using a hand blender, dissolve SODIUM ALGINATE in water. Let sit for 15 minutes, then warm briefly in a microwave oven.

04 Unmold frozen yogurt spheres in alginate bath. Let sit for 3 minutes while gently stirring once in a while to prevent the spheres from touching.

05 Fill a medium-sized bowl with water. Using a slotted spoon, delicately collect the spheres and briefly rinse them in the water, then remove excess water from each sphere by applying a piece of paper towel on the bottom of the spoon. Reserve.

ASSEMBLY

06 Serve salad and spheres on top of shiso leaves. Decorate each plate with raspberries and pistachios.

AVANT-GARDE BEER TASTING

DIFFICULTY   3/5
ACTIVE TIME   1:00
TOTAL TIME   1:00
*TIPS ON FOAM   P. 56

INGREDIENTS

BEER JELLIES

1 ½ cups (375 ml) pale ale
1 ½ cups (375 ml) red ale
1 ½ cups (375 ml) black ale
6 tbs (90 ml) honey
3 sachets (6 g) AGAR-AGAR

CHEDDARY CROUTONS (OPTIONAL)

1 baguette
20 cheddar slices
1 onion
1 tbs (15 ml) butter
pinch of salt
pinch of pepper
2 tbs (30 ml) beer

BEER FOAM

⅕ cup (50 ml) beer
1 sachet (2 g) SOY LECITHIN

TO SERVE

cheese

DIRECTIONS

BEER JELLIES

 01 In a small pot, bring pale ale, 2 tbs honey and 1 sachet AGAR-AGAR to a boil while stirring. Remove from heat and let sit for 5 minutes.

 02 Pour cooled preparation into glasses of various shapes and sizes or into ice trays and refrigerate for 10 minutes. Delicately unmold, then set aside. Repeat this step with red and black ales (or make all three jellies at once to save time).

CHEDDARY CROUTONS (OPTIONAL)

 03 Preheat oven to 400 °F (200 °C). Slice baguette into croutons and brush with oil, then place on a baking sheet. Slice onion into half-moons.

 04 Bake croutons in the oven for 5-10 minutes. While you wait, heat butter in a small pan on medium heat, then cook onion in the butter with salt and pepper for 2 minutes. Deglaze with 2 tbs (30 ml) beer.

 05 Top each baked crouton with a few onion slices and a slice of cheddar and put back in the oven until the cheese has melted.

BEER FOAM*

 06 In a rectangular, flat-bottomed bowl, pour beer and sprinkle in SOY LECITHIN. Then, using a hand blender, dissolve soy lecithin into the solution. Mix for 3 to 4 minutes, then let sit for 5 minutes.

 07 To serve, collect foam with a spoon. To obtain more foam, repeat step 6.

ASSEMBLY

 08 Arrange jellies and cheddary croutons on cutting boards. Top jellies with foam and serve with a knife. Alternatively, simply serve foam-topped jellies with fresh croutons and cheese.

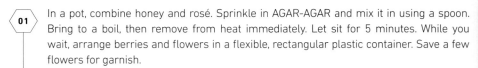

HONEY-GOLD
ROSÉ JELLY

DIFFICULTY 1/5
ACTIVE TIME 0:10
TOTAL TIME 1:10

INGREDIENTS

1 ½ cups (375 ml) rosé
5 tbs (75 ml) honey
1 cup (250 ml) berries
1 cup (250 ml) edible flowers
1 sachet (2 g) AGAR-AGAR

TO SERVE

6 cherries
cheese
croutons

DIRECTIONS

01 In a pot, combine honey and rosé. Sprinkle in AGAR-AGAR and mix it in using a spoon. Bring to a boil, then remove from heat immediately. Let sit for 5 minutes. While you wait, arrange berries and flowers in a flexible, rectangular plastic container. Save a few flowers for garnish.

02 Pour preparation into prepared container and let sit in the refrigerator for 1 hour.

ASSEMBLY

03 Serve as pictured, topped with cherries and a few flowers, with a cheese platter and croutons.

Sa | Cl | ▦ | 🥄 | Aa

BERRY
MONTAGE

DIFFICULTY   3/5
ACTIVE TIME   0:25
TOTAL TIME   1:05
*TIPS ON SPHERES   P. 46

INGREDIENTS

ALMOND LIQUEUR SPHERES

a few currants
a few bluberries
⅔ cup (170 ml) almond liqueur
2 cups (500 ml) water
½ tsp (2.5 ml) CALCIUM LACTATE
1 sachet (2 g) SODIUM ALGINATE

RASPBERRY & BASIL JAM

2 cups (500 ml) raspeberries
½ cup (125 ml) sugar
½ lemon
½ orange
1 tbs (15 ml) lemon juice
10 basil leaves
1 sachet (2 g) AGAR-AGAR

TO SERVE

sunflower shoots
mâche
olive oil
zest
cheese
croutons

DIRECTIONS

ALMOND LIQUEUR SPHERES*

01 Warm up 1 tbs (15 ml) of water and combine with CALCIUM LACTATE. Stir until the calcium lactate is fully diluted, then combine with almond liqueur. Place currants and blueberries in small, demi-spherical molds (1 piece of fruit per mold).

02 Pour mixture into prepared molds and let sit in the freezer for 1 hour or until the spheres are frozen. (While you wait, make RASPBERRY & BASIL JAM.)

03 In a rectangular, flat-bottomed bowl and using a hand blender, dissolve SODIUM ALGINATE in remaining water. Let sit for 15 minutes, then warm briefly in a microwave oven.

04 Unmold frozen liqueur spheres in alginate bath. Let sit for 3 minutes while gently stirring once in a while to prevent the spheres from touching.

05 Fill a medium-sized bowl with water. Using a slotted spoon, delicately collect the spheres and briefly rinse them in the water, then remove excess water from each sphere by applying a piece of paper towel on the bottom of the spoon. Reserve.

RASPBERRY & BASIL JAM

06 First, zest lemon and orange (you will not need the actual fruit) Save about a teaspoon's worth (5 ml) for the next part of the recipe and use the rest in this section.

07 In a pot, bring all ingredients except for the basil to a boil and cook for 10 minutes. Finely chop basil while you wait. After 10 minutes, remove from heat, add in basil and blend with a hand blender until homogenous. Sprinkle in AGAR-AGAR and blend for 5 more seconds, then put back on the heat, bring to a boil and remove from heat immediately.

08 Pour mixture into small plastic containers or molds and refrigerate for 20 minutes, then unmold.

ASSEMBLY

09 Serve jam on a bed of shoots, mâche and zest with a drizzle of olive oil. Top with a liqueur sphere. Serve alongside a cheese platter and croutons.

MODERNIZED SAVOURY PARFAIT

DIFFICULTY	2/5
ACTIVE TIME	0:45
TOTAL TIME	0:45
*TIPS ON FOAM	P. 56

INGREDIENTS

ONION & MASCARPONE ESPUMA

1 cup (250 ml) heavy cream
½ cup (125 ml) mascarpone
1 onion
a dash olive oil
sea salt, to taste

TOMATO TARTARES

2 red tomatoes
2 yellow tomatoes
1 shallot
1 tbs (15 ml) capers
parsley, to taste
basil, to taste
1 egg yolk
a few drops Tabasco
a few drops Worcestershire sauce
1 tsp (5 ml) Dijon mustard
2 tbs (30 ml) grapeseed oil
salt, to taste
pepper, to taste

RADISH FOAM

12 large radishes
1 sachet (2 g) SOY LECITHIN

TO SERVE

a few radishes

DIRECTIONS

ONION & MASCARPONE ESPUMA

 In a small pan, cook chopped onion in oil for 2 minutes. Season and reserve.

 In a pot, warm cream on medium-low heat. Stir in mascarpone and onion and cook for 3 more minutes. Filter through a sieve to get rid of the onions as well as any clumps.

 Pour filtered preparation into a culinary whipper. Shut the whipper, charge an N2O cartridge and shake for 5 seconds. Refrigerate the siphon for 30 minutes before serving.

TOMATO TARTARES

 First, remove stems from tomatoes and blanch them. Peel, seed and dice the tomatoes while keeping the red ones separate from the yellow ones. Place the red tomatoes in a mixing bowl and the yellow ones in another.

 Finely chop shallot, halve capers and chop herbs. Divide all these between the two bowls and mix in well. Season. In a small bowl, whisk together egg yolk, Tabasco, Worcestershire sauce, mustard and oil. Once again, divide between the two mixing bowls. Reserve.

RADISH **FOAM***

 Use a juicer to extract juice from radishes. Filter. Pour 1 ½ cups (375 ml) radish juice into a flat-bottomed, rectangular bowl. Sprinkle in SOY LECITHN. Using a hand blender, blend for 3 to 4 minutes, then let sit for 5 minutes.

 To serve, collect foam using a spoon. If needed and to obtain more foam, repeat step 6.

ASSEMBLY

 Serve in clear glasses as pictured: first, a layer of espuma, followed by a layer of yellow tartare; second, another layer of espuma followed by a layer of red tartare; lastly, top with radish foam and one whole radish.

DECONSTRUCTED COCOA

DIFFICULTY   3/5
ACTIVE TIME   0:15
TOTAL TIME   0:15
*TIPS ON CAVIAR   P. 42

INGREDIENTS

COCOA CAVIAR

1 ¼ cups (315 ml) water
1 oz (30 g) sugar
1 oz (30 g) cocoa powder
2 cups (500 ml) water
1 sachet (2 g) SODIUM ALGINATE
1 sachet (5 g) CALCIUM LACTATE

WHITE CHOCOLATE CREAM

1 ¼ cups (315 ml) 35% cooking cream
3.5 oz white chocolate, chopped

DIRECTIONS

COCOA **CAVIAR***

01 In a pan, bring the sugar, cocoa powder and 1 ¼ cups (315 ml) water to a boil and continue cooking for 2 minutes.

02 In a rectangular, flat-bottomed bowl and using a hand blender, dissolve 1 sachet of SODIUM ALGINATE in the cocoa praparation. Let sit for 10 minutes.

03 Dissolve 1 sachet of CALCIUM LACTATE in 2 cups (500 ml) of water using a spoon. Then, using a pipette held at a 90° angle, slowly drip droplets of the alginate solution into the calcium lactate bath. Let sit for 3 minutes, then empty the calcium lactate bath into the sink and onto a sieve so you're left with just the cocoa caviar. Rinse in lukewarm water.

WHITE CHOCOLATE CREAM

04 Bring the cream to a boil and pour it into a bowl with the white chocolate; stir, then set aside until cool.

ASSEMBLY

05 Pour the white chocolate cream into serving spoons, top with some cocoa caviar and serve.

CHIA PUDDING
WITH FRUIT CAVIAR

DIFFICULTY 2/5
ACTIVE TIME 0:45
TOTAL TIME 1:45
*TIPS ON PEARLS P. 22

INGREDIENTS

2 tall glasses filled with oil

CHIA PUDDING

2 tbs (30 ml) chia seeds
1 cup (250 ml) soymilk

STRAWBERRY PEARLS

2 cups (500 ml) strawberries
1 ¾ cups (440 ml) water
1 cup (250 ml) sugar
1 sachet (2 g) AGAR-AGAR

ORANGE PEARLS

1 cup (250 ml) orange juice
1 sachet (2 g) AGAR-AGAR

TO GARNISH

goji berries
puffed rice
orange zest

NOTE

You can replace the soymilk with your
favorite plant-based milk.

DIRECTIONS

01 Refrigerate both glasses of oil until very cold, or, to save time, place it in the freezer for 1 hour.

CHIA PUDDING

02 Combine all ingredients and transfer to small, clear bowls. Let sit in the refrigerator for at least 30 minutes before serving. While you wait, make strawberry and orange pearls.

STRAWBERRY **PEARLS***

03 Cut strawberries into small pieces, place them in a medium-sized pot and cover with water. Cover the pot and bring to a boil, then let simmer for another 20 minutes. Regularly scoop off any foam forming on the surface.

04 Using a sieve and above a medium-sized bowl, filter preparation without pressing the strawberries. Discard strawberries, then transfer filtered liquid back to the pot and add in sugar. While stirring, bring back to a boil to completely dissolve the sugar, then let simmer for another 5 minutes. Again, regularly scoop off any foam forming on the surface.

05 Sprinkle 1 sachet AGAR-AGAR into the pot and mix it in using a spoon. Bring to a boil one last time, then remove from heat immediately.

06 Remove one glass of cold oil from the freezer or refrigerator. Using a pipette held at a 90° angle, slowly drip droplets of the agar-agar preparation into the cold oil. Stir gently, then, using a sieve, collect pearls and briefly rinse them under water. Reserve.

ORANGE **PEARLS***

07 In a small pot, reduce orange juice until only about ¾ of a cup (190 ml) of liquid remains. Sprinkle in 1 sachet AGAR-AGAR and mix it in using a spoon. Bring to a boil, then immediately remove from the heat.

08 Remove remaining glass of cold oil from the freezer or refrigerator. Using a pipette held at a 90° angle, slowly drip droplets of the agar-agar preparation into the cold oil. Stir gently, then, using a sieve, collect pearls and briefly rinse them under water.

ASSEMBLY

09 Mix strawberry and orange pearls into each pudding, then decorate with goji berries, puffed rice and orange zest.

VOLATILE
DESSERT ASPIC

DIFFICULTY   1/5
ACTIVE TIME   0:10
TOTAL TIME   0:40

INGREDIENTS

1 ½ cups (375 ml) white port
½ cup (125 ml) edible flowers
1 tbs (15 ml) maple syrup
1 sachet (2 g) AGAR-AGAR

TO SERVE

goosebery syrup
white gooseberries
orange zest
mint leaves
lychee aroma by MOLECULE-R

DIRECTIONS

01 In a pot, combine maple syrup and port. Sprinkle in AGAR-AGAR and mix it in using a spoon. Bring to a boil, then remove from heat immediately. Let sit for 5 minutes. While you wait, place flowers in small, rectangular molds (1 to 2 flowers per compartment).

02 Pour preparation into prepared molds and let sit in the refrigerator for 30 minutes.

ASSEMBLY

03 Chop mint leaves. Drip a droplet or 2 of lychee aroma onto a piece of blotting paper inserted in an AROMASPOON™ by MOLECULE-R. In the spoon, place some gooseberry syrup. Then, in each serving spoon, place a wine jelly and decorate with orange zest and mint. When taking a bite, keep the AROMASPOON close to your nose while chewing. Inhale the lychee aroma and experience volatile flavoring!

MAPLE TRIPTYCH

DIFFICULTY   3/5
ACTIVE TIME   1:10
TOTAL TIME   1:10
*TIPS ON PEARLS   P. 22

INGREDIENTS

1 tall glass filled with oil

RAW NUT BROWNIE

3 cups (750 ml) chopped medjool dates
⅓ cup (85 ml) cashews
¼ cup (65 ml) hazelnuts
¼ cup (65 ml) almonds
2 tbsp (60 ml) raw cocoa
salt, to taste

MAPLE TILES

⅓ cup (85 ml) water
⅔ cup (170 ml) maple syrup
a few cilantro sprigs
1 sachet (2 g) AGAR-AGAR

MAPLE PEARLS

¾ cup (190 ml) maple syrup
¼ cup (65 ml) water
1 sachet (2 g) AGAR-AGAR

MAPLE BUTTER

½ cup (125 ml) maple syrup
¾ cup (190 ml) packed brown sugar
1 egg yolk
½ tsp (2.5 ml) vanilla extract
pinch of salt

TO SERVE

fruit

DIRECTIONS

 01 Refrigerate glass of oil overnight, or, to save time, place it in the freezer for 1 hour.

RAW NUT BROWNIE

 02 First, pit dates and place them in a food processor. Add in cashews, cocoa and salt and blend until homogenous. Add hazelnuts and almonds and blend some more, until the nuts are mixed into the paste but still chunky. Transfer to a rectangular baking dish and refrigerate for 30 minutes before cutting into squares.

MAPLE TILES

 03 Combine water and maple syrup and sprinkle with 1 sachet of AGAR-AGAR. Bring to a boil, then remove from heat immediately.

 04 Pour a small amount of the preparation onto a plate and into a thin layer. Tilt the plate as you pour to cover as much surface as possible. Refrigerate the plate and repeat. Take out of the refrigerator 10 minutes before serving so the cannellonis can warm up and cut them into small rectangles using a knife.

MAPLE **PEARLS***

 05 Combine maple syrup and water in a pot. Sprinkle in remaining sachet of AGAR-AGAR. Bring to a boil, then remove from heat immediately.

 06 Take glass of oil out of the refrigerator. Using a pipette held at a 90° angle, slowly drip droplets of the agar-agar preparation into the oil. Pour into a sieve above the sink to discard the oil. Rinse under cold water and reserve.

MAPLE BUTTER

07 In a bain-marie, combine all ingredients and bring to a boil. Whisk using an egg beater until spikes start forming (5 to 7 minutes). Remove from heat and whisk in vanilla.

ASSEMBLY

 08 Divide brownie squares, maple tiles, maple pearls and maple butter between plates. Serve with fruit.

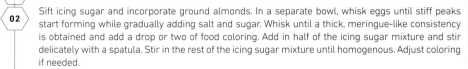

FRENCH NEW WAVE

DIFFICULTY   4/5
ACTIVE TIME   1:30
TOTAL TIME   2:00
*TIPS ON FOAM   P. 56
*TIPS ON CAVIAR   P. 42

INGREDIENTS

MACARON SHELL

1 ¼ cup (315 ml) icing sugar
1 ¼ cup (315 ml) finely ground almonds
3 egg whites
2 tbsp (60 ml) powdered sugar
pinch of salt
red food coloring

RASPBERRY WHIPPED CREAM

4 cups (1l) frozen raspberries
¾ cup (190 ml) powdered sugar
½ cup (125 ml) water
2 cups (500 ml) heavy cream

ROSE CAVIAR

1 ½ cups (375 ml) rosewater
2 cups (500 ml) water
1 sachet (2 g) SODIUM ALGINATE
1 sachet (5 g) CALCIUM LACTATE

ROSE ICING

⅔ cup (170 ml) butter at room temperature
2 cups (500 ml) powdered sugar
1 tbs (15 ml) rosewater

LIME FOAM

1 ½ cups (375 ml) lime juice
1 sachet (2 g) SOY LECITHIN

TO SERVE

raspberries
dragon fruit pieces

DIRECTIONS

MACARON SHELLS

01 Line a baking sheet with parchment paper.

02 Sift icing sugar and incorporate ground almonds. In a separate bowl, whisk eggs until stiff peaks start forming while gradually adding salt and sugar. Whisk until a thick, meringue-like consistency is obtained and add a drop or two of food coloring. Add in half of the icing sugar mixture and stir delicately with a spatula. Stir in the rest of the icing sugar mixture until homogenous. Adjust coloring if needed.

03 Using a pastry bag, pipe macaron batter buttons onto the baking sheet, leaving 2 inches (5 cm) between each button. Let sit for 30 minutes, then cook in the oven at 300 °F (150 °C) for 20 to 25 minutes or until shells are firm (make RASPBERRY WHIPPED CREAM and ROSE CAVIAR while you wait). Let cool completely before serving (Make ROSE ICING and LIME FOAM while you wait).

RASPBERRY WHIPPED CREAM

04 Bring frozen raspberries, sugar and water to a boil while stirring. Simmer for 5 minutes and remove from heat. Whisk the mixture, then, pour through a fine sieve and into a bowl. Let cool (Make ROSE CAVIAR while you wait).

05 Once cooled, whisk cream until stiff peaks start forming. Gently incorporate raspberry syrup. Refrigerate until serving time.

ROSE CAVIAR*

06 Bring rosewater to a boil and remove from heat. In a blender, combine with SODIUM ALGINATE and let cool down at room temperature.

07 In a bowl, mix CALCIUM LACTATE into water until fully dissolved. Using a pipette held at a 90° angle, drip droplets of the alginate preparation into the calcium lactate bath. Let sit for 3 minutes, then pour into a sieve above to sink to discard the calcium water. Rinse caviar and reserve in the refrigerator, in a little bit of rosewater.

ROSE ICING

08 In a bowl, using an egg beater, whisk together butter and sugar until smooth. Add in rosewater as needed to loosen texture.

LIME FOAM*

09 In a rectangular, flat-bottomed bowl, combine water and lime juice and sprinkle in SOY LECITHIN. Using a hand blender, blend for 3 to 4 minutes, then let sit for 5 minutes. If needed and to obtain more foam, repeat this step.

ASSEMBLY

10 Serve on dark-colored plates. First, spread a bit of icing on each macaron and spread generously on each plate as well. Place iced macarons on plates, iced facing up. Top with a few raspberries and a piece of dragon fruit. Garnish each plate with whipped cream and lime foam. Top lime cloud with rosewater caviar.

ENCAPSULATED DAIQUIRI

DIFFICULTY   3/5
ACTIVE TIME   0:20
TOTAL TIME   1:20
*TIPS ON FOAM   P. 56
*TIPS ON SPHERES P. 46

INGREDIENTS

STRAWBERRY COULIS SPHERES

2 cups (500 ml) strawberries
2 tbs (30 ml) sugar
2 cups (500 ml) water
½ tsp (2.5 ml) CALCIUM LACTATE
1 sachet (2 g) SODIUM ALGINATE

STRAWBERRY & RHUBARB FOAM

¾ cup (190 ml) sugar
3 cups (750 ml) fresh rhubarb
1 cup (250 ml) strawberries
juice of half a lemon
2 cups (500 ml) water
1 sachet (2 g) SOY LECITHIN

TO GARNISH

rhubarb sticks cut into pieces 3 inches long
lemon-flavored sparkling water

NOTE

This cocktail is delicious as a virgin, but if you'd like to, feel free to mix 1 fl oz (30 ml) white rum with the sparkling water in a cocktail shaker before assembling.

You can replace the 3 cups (750 ml) of fresh rhubarb by 450 g of frozen one.

DIRECTIONS

STRAWBERRY COULIS SPHERES*

01 In a blender, puree strawberries, sugar and CALCIUM LACTATE. Pour mixture into small, demi-spherical molds and let sit in the freezer for 1 hour or until the spheres are frozen.

02 In a rectangular, flat-bottomed bowl and using a hand blender, dissolve SODIUM ALGINATE in water. Let sit for 15 minutes.

03 Unmold frozen coulis spheres in alginate bath. Let sit for 3 minutes while gently stirring once in a while to prevent the spheres from touching.

04 Fill a medium-sized bowl with water. Using a slotted spoon, delicately collect the spheres and briefly rinse them in the water, then remove excess water from each sphere by applying a piece of paper towel on the bottom of the spoon. Reserve.

STRAWBERRY & RHUBARB FOAM*

05 In a pot, bring water and sugar to a boil. Add rhubarb coarsely chopped and strawberries, mix and leave to simmer on low heat for 7 minutes.

06 Using a sieve and above a medium-sized bowl, filter the mixture without pressing the solid ingredients, which can then be discarded. Mix in lemon juice.

07 In a rectangular, flat-bottomed bowl, transfer approximately 1 ½ cups (375 ml) of filtered mixture and sprinkle in SOY LECITHIN. Using a hand blender, blend for 3 to 4 minutes, then let sit for 5 minutes.

08 To serve, collect foam using a spoon. If needed and to obtain more foam, repeat step 7.

ASSEMBLY

09 Fill a glass with cold lemon-flavored sparkling water. In this glass, place a strawberry coulis sphere and a piece of rhubarb. Top with strawberry and rhubarb foam and serve.

HONEY CAVIAR & ROSE DICE

INGREDIENTS

tall glass of oil

ROSE WATER DICE

1 cup (250 ml) rose water
2 tbs (30 ml) cane sugar
1 sachet (2 g) AGAR-AGAR

AGAVE PEARLS

½ cup (125 ml) agave syrup
⅓ cup (85 ml) water
1 sachet (2 g) AGAR-AGAR

TO SERVE

1 grapefruit
1 navel orange
1 pomelo
1 tangerine
lavender flowers
olive oil
pepper
black sea salt
edible capucine leaves

DIRECTIONS

 01 Place the tall glass of oil in the refrigerator to cool overnight, or, to save time, place it in the freezer for 1 hour.

ROSE WATER DICE

 02 In a pot, bring rose water and cane sugar to a boil with 1 sachet AGAR-AGAR, then remove from heat immediately. Pour into a rectangular plastic container and refrigerate for 30 minutes. (Make AGAVE PEARLS while you wait.) Unmold, dice and reserve.

AGAVE **PEARLS***

 03 In a pot, bring agave syrup and water to a boil with 1 sachet AGAR-AGAR, then remove from heat immediately.

 04 Remove oil from the freezer or refrigerator. Using a pipette held at a 90° angle, slowly drip droplets of the agar-agar preparation in the cold oil. Pour onto a sieve and above the sink to get rid of the oil and rinse under cold water. Set aside.

ASSEMBLY

 05 First, cut citrus fruit into supremes. Divide rose water dice between ramekins, then, top each ramekin with agave pearls, supremes and flowers. Sprinkle with pepper and sea salt and finish with a dash of oil and a capucine leaf planted in each ramekin.

DECONSTRUCTED MOJITO

DIFFICULTY   2/5
ACTIVE TIME   0:20
TOTAL TIME   1:20
*TIPS ON CAVIAR   P. 42
*TIPS ON FOAM   P. 56

INGREDIENTS

BLUEBERRY CAVIAR

1 cup (250 ml) water
1 cup (250 ml) blueberries
4 tbs (60 ml) sugar
1 sachet (2 g) SODIUM ALGINATE
1 sachet (5 g) CALCIUM LACTATE

LAVENDER FOAM

1 ½ cups (375 ml) water
3 bags lavender tea
1 sachet (2 g) SOY LECITHIN

TO SERVE

2 fl oz (60 ml) white rum
1 fl oz (30 ml) club soda
1 fl oz (30 ml) lime juice
2 tsp (10 ml) sugar

TO GARNISH

fresh mint leaves

DIRECTIONS

BLUEBERRY CAVIAR*

 01 In a pot, bring 1 cup (250 ml) of water to a boil. Mix blueberries and sugar in and continue boiling for 2 minutes while stirring constantly.

 02 In a rectangular, flat-bottomed bowl and using a hand blender, dissolve 1 sachet of SODIUM ALGINATE in blueberry puree. Let sit for 10 minutes.

 03 Remove from heat and blend. If you have an immersion blender, you can do this directly in the pot; if not, either let the mixture cool down a bit before you transfer it to your blender, or be extra careful not to let steam build up too much in the blender as you blend.

 04 Dissolve 1 sachet of CALCIUM LACTATE in 2 cups (500 ml) of water using a spoon. Then, using a pipette held at a 90° angle, slowly drip droplets of the alginate solution into the calcium lactate bath. Let sit for 3 minutes, then empty the calcium lactate bath into the sink and onto a sieve so you're left with just the blueberry caviar. Rinse in lukewarm water.

LAVENDER FOAM*

 05 Bring water to a boil and remove from heat. Place tea bags in hot water and let sit for 5 minutes.

 06 In a rectangular, flat-bottomed bowl, pour tea and sprinkle in SOY LECITHIN. Using a hand blender, blend for 3 to 4 minutes, then let sit for 5 minutes.

 07 To serve, collect foam using a spoon. If needed and to obtain more foam, repeat step 5.

ASSEMBLY

 08 In a cocktail shaker, shake together rum, club soda and lime juice. Pour into a glass and add in a few blueberry pearls. Top first with a few mint leaves, then with the lavender foam, and serve.

AVANT-GARDE CREME BRULEE

DIFFICULTY   4/5
ACTIVE TIME   1:00
TOTAL TIME   2:00
*TIPS ON PEARLS   P. 22

INGREDIENTS

1 tall glass of oil

CREME BRULEE

7/8 cup (215 ml) dark chocolate
½ cup (125 ml) milk chocolate
2 cups (500 ml) half and half
1 bag Earl Grey
8 egg yolks
¼ cup (65 ml) cane sugar
2 cups (500 ml) heavy cream
¼ cup (65 ml) brown sugar

VANILLA PEARLS

1 cup (250 ml) half and half
2 tbs (30 ml) cane sugar
2 vanilla cloves
1 sachet (2 g) AGAR-AGAR

TO GARNISH

blueberries
blackberries
wildflowers
thyme sprigs

DIRECTIONS

01 Refrigerate oil until very cold, or, to save time, place it in the freezer for 1 hour.

CREME BRULEE

02 Chop chocolate, preheat oven to 300 °F (150 °C) and arrange ramekins on a baking sheet.

03 In a medium-sized pot, bring half and half to a boil, then remove from heat and put tea bag in. Cover and let steep for 4 minutes.

04 Using a sieve, filter cream tea (discard the bag). In a medium-sized bowl and using a whisk, gently combine yolks, cane sugar and heavy cream. Then, while whisking, incorporate about a quarter of the tea. Wait 1 minute, then incorporate the remaining tea.

05 Pour preparation into ramekins and cook in the oven for 45 minutes or until a knife comes out clean. Once cooked, transfer ramekins to a cooling rack and let cool down at room temperature for at least 2 hours. (Make VANILLA PEARLS while the creme brulees are cooking or cooling.)

06 Sprinkle each creme brulee with brown sugar, then caramelize using a torch. Serve as soon as possible after caramelizing.

VANILLA PEARLS*

07 In a small pot, heat cream and sugar without boiling and infuse vanilla for a minute. Remove from heat and infuse for 15 more minutes.

08 Put the pot back on the heat. Incorporate AGAR-AGAR while stirring and bring to a boil, then remove from heat immediately.

09 Remove oil from freezer or refrigerator. Using a pipette held at a 90° angle, slowly drip droplets of the agar-agar preparation in the cold oil. Stir gently, then, using a slotted spoon, delicately collect pearls and briefly rinse them in water. Remove excess water from each spoonful by applying a piece of paper towel on the bottom of the spoon. Reserve.

ASSEMBLY

10 Decorate each creme brulee as pictured and serve.

Sa Cl ⊞ 🥄

PUMPKIN PIE, REVISITED

INGREDIENTS

STRAWBERRY COULIS SPHERES

2 tbs (30 ml) water
¾ cup (190 ml) sugar
1 cup (250 ml) whipping cream
3 eggs
1 cup (250 ml) pumpkin puree
1 tsp (5 ml) ground cinnamon
1 tsp (5 ml) ground ginger
2 tbs (30 ml) lukewarm milk
2 cups (500 ml) water
1 tsp (5 ml) CALCIUM LACTATE
1 sachet (2 g) SODIUM ALGINATE

PIE CRUST

1 cup (250 ml) quick cooking oats
¼ cup (65 ml) unbleached flour
¼ cup (65 ml) brown sugar
¼ cup (65 ml) unsalted butter

VANILLA ICING

2 cups (500 ml) icing sugar
2 tbs (30 ml) unsalted butter
2 tbs (30 ml) milk
½ tsp (2.5 ml) vanilla extract

TO GARNISH

¼ cup (65 ml) pumpkin seeds
allspice

DIRECTIONS

PUMPKIN PIE **SPHERES***

01 Preheat oven to 300 °F (150 °C). In a pot, bring 2 tbs (30 ml) of water and ½ cup (125 ml) of sugar to a boil while stirring. Cook just until mixture starts browning, then remove from heat. Gradually incorporate cream while stirring and set aside to cool.

02 In a bowl, whisk eggs together with the rest of the sugar. Mix in pumpkin puree, cinnamon, ginger and cooled caramel. Transfer to a baking dish and cook in the oven for about 30 minutes or until the edges are firm and the middle is still slightly wobbly. Set aside.

03 Blend together milk and CALCIUM LACTATE, then transfer cooked pie filling to blender and blend some more until homogenous. If the mixture is too thick to blend, add in more warm milk.

04 Divide the mixture between small, demi-spherical molds and let sit in the freezer for 1 hour or until the spheres are frozen. While you wait, make pie crust.

05 In a rectangular, flat-bottomed bowl and using a hand blender, dissolve SODIUM ALGINATE in water. Let sit for 15 minutes.

06 Unmold frozen pumpkin pie spheres in alginate bath. Let sit for 3 minutes while gently stirring once in a while to prevent the spheres from touching.

07 Fill a medium-sized bowl with remaining water. Using a slotted spoon, delicately collect the spheres and briefly rinse them in the water, then remove excess water from each sphere by applying a piece of paper towel on the bottom of the spoon. Reserve.

PIE CRUST

08 Move a rack to the bottom third of your oven, then preheat to 350 °F (180 °C). Soften butter, then, in a bowl, combine oats, flour and brown sugar, then incorporate sugar. Transfer to an 8" (20 cm) square baking dish and cook for 30 minutes, then set aside to cool. Cut into 4 by 4" (10 x 10 cm) squares once cooled.

VANILLA ICING

09 Soften butter in a small pan or in the microwave. In a bowl, combine confectioner's sugar, butter, milk and vanilla until homogenous and fluffy. Transfer icing to a pastry bag.

ASSEMBLY

10 Toast and crush the pumpkin seeds. Place each pie crust on a ramekin or small plate, then top with a pumpkin pie sphere and decorate as pictured with icing, seeds and allspice.

MELON BALL

INGREDIENTS

ORANGE SPHERES

⅔ cup (170 ml)s orange juice
2 cups (500 ml) water
½ tsp (2.5 ml) **CALCIUM LACTATE**
1 sachet (2 g) **SODIUM ALGINATE**

TO SERVE

melon liqueur (midori)
orange zest

DIRECTIONS

ORANGE **SPHERES***

 01 In a bowl, dissolve CALCIUM LACTATE into orange juice. Pour mixture into small, demi-spherical molds and let sit in the freezer for 1 hour or until the spheres are frozen.

 02 In a rectangular, flat-bottomed bowl and using a hand blender, dissolve SODIUM ALGINATE in water. Let sit for 15 minutes, then warm briefly in a microwave oven.

 03 Unmold frozen orange spheres in alginate bath. Let sit for 3 minutes while gently stirring once in a while to prevent the spheres from touching.

 04 Fill a medium-sized bowl with water. Using a slotted spoon, delicately collect the spheres and briefly rinse them in the water, then remove excess water from each sphere by applying a piece of paper towel on the bottom of the spoon. Reserve.

ASSEMBLY

 05 To serve, put each orange sphere in a tasting spoon. Add a dash of melon liqueur in each spoon and decorate with orange zest.

RED
DECADENCE

INGREDIENTS

CHOCOLATE CAKE

1 ¼ cups (315 ml) all-purpose flour
¾ cup (190 ml) sugar
1 tsp (5 ml) baking soda
½ tsp (2.5 ml) sea salt
¾ cup (190 ml) buttermilk
¼ cup (65 ml) grapeseed oil
½ tsp (2.5 ml) vanilla extract
⅛ cup (30 ml) unsweetened chocolate
½ cup (125 ml) semi-sweet dark chocolate

RASPBERRY GLAZE

3 cups (750 ml) raspberry liqueur
¾ cup (190 ml) seedless raspberry jam

CRANBERRY SPHERE

1 cup (250 ml) pure cranberry juice
2 tbs (30 ml) maple syrup
2 cups (500 ml) water
½ tsp (2.5 ml) CALCIUM LACTATE
1 sachet (2 g) SODIUM ALGINATE

RASPBERRY FOAM

3 cups (750 ml) raspberries
¼ cup (65 ml) water
2 tbs (30 ml) sugar
1 sachet (2 g) SOY LECITHIN

BASIL WHIPPED CREAM

2 cups (500 ml) cold heavy cream
20 basil leaves
pinch of salt

TO SERVE

chocolate shavings
dark chocolate pieces

DIRECTIONS

CHOCOLATE CUPCAKES

 01 Preheat oven to 375 °F. (190 °C) Line a muffin tin with paper liners. In a large bowl, whisk together flour, sugar, baking soda and salt. In a separate bowl, combine buttermilk, oil and vanilla. Pour onto dry ingredients, along with chocolate (melted and chopped). Whisk until homogenous. Transfer batter to prepared muffin tins and cook in the oven for 17 minutes or until a toothpick inserted in the center comes out clean.

RASPBERRY GLAZE

 02 Bring raspberry liqueur to a boil in a small pot. Reduce by half on medium heat. Transfer ½ a cup (125 ml) reduced liqueur to a bowl and reserve at room temperature. Reserve remainder in the pot.

 03 Peel muffin liners off of cupcakes and transfer the cupcakes to a large serving plate. Brush cupcake tops with 1 tbs (15 ml) each of raspberry reduction from the bowl. Put the remaining raspberry reduction from the bowl back in the pot and bring to a boil. Reduce to a thick syrup on medium heat. Brush cupcakes with glaze in a few layers, giving the cake time to absorb the glaze between each layer.

CRANBERRY SPHERES*

 04 Reduce juice to ½ a cup. Mix in maple syrup and CALCIUM LACTATE. Pour mixture into small, demi-spherical molds and let sit in the freezer for 1 hour or until frozen. (While you wait, make RASPBERRY EMULSION and BASIL WHIPPED CREAM.)

 05 In a rectangular, flat-bottomed bowl and using a hand blender, dissolve SODIUM ALGINATE in water. Let sit for 15 minutes, then warm briefly in a microwave oven.

 06 Unmold frozen spheres in alginate bath. Let sit for 3 minutes while gently stirring once in a while to prevent the spheres from touching.

 07 Fill a medium-sized bowl with water. Using a slotted spoon, delicately collect the spheres and briefly rinse them in the water, then remove excess water from each sphere by applying a piece of paper towel on the bottom of the spoon. Reserve.

RASPBERRY FOAM*

 08 Before you start, place a large mixing bowl in the freezer (this is for the next part of the recipe). Then, using a juicer, extract juice from raspberries. Filter ¾ of a cup (190 ml) of juice.

 09 In a rectangular, flat-bottomed bowl, combine filtered juice, water and sugar and sprinkle in SOY LECITHIN. Using a hand blender, blend for 3 to 4 minutes, then let sit for 5 minutes. If needed and to obtain more foam, repeat this step.

BASIL WHIPPED CREAM

 10 Take the mixing bowl out of the freezer. Combine all ingredients in a blender, then transfer to the bowl and mix, using an electric mixer, until frothy. Refrigerate until serving time.

ASSEMBLY

 11 Serve cupcakes and cranberry spheres topped with basil whipped cream and raspberry emulsion. Sprinkle with chocolate shavings and finish with a piece of dark chocolate.

MOUSSE QUINTET

DIFFICULTY	1/5
ACTIVE TIME	0:45
TOTAL TIME	2:45
*TIPS ON FOAM	P. 56

INGREDIENTS

DARK CHOCOLATE MOUSSE

⅔ cup (170 ml) semi-sweetened chocolate
2 tbs (30 ml) unsalted butter
2 eggs
1 ½ cups (375 ml) heavy cream
2 tbs (30 ml) sugar

WHITE CHOCOLATE MOUSSE

⅔ cup (170 ml) white chocolate
½ vanilla clove
1 cup (250 ml) heavy cream
4 eggs
⅓ cup (85 ml) sugar

MATCHA-GREEN TEA FOAM

1 ½ cups (375 ml) water
4 green tea bags
4 tsp (60 ml) matcha powder
1 sachet (2 g) SOY LECITHIN

HIBISCUS-POMEGRANATE FOAM

1 cup (250 ml) pomegranate seeds
1 ½ cups (375 ml) water
4 hibiscus tea bags
1 sachet (2 g) SOY LECITHIN

GRAPEFRUIT FOAM

1 ½ cups (375 ml) grapefruit juice
1 sachet (2 g) SOY LECITHIN

NOTE

All three "FOAM" recipes can be made at
the same time.

DIRECTIONS

DARK CHOCOLATE MOUSSE

 01 Coarsely chop dark chocolate. Crack eggs and discard whites. Reserve yolks for the next step. Wash and reserve cracked shells for serving.

 02 Melt chocolate in a bain-marie, then remove from heat. Whisk in egg yolks until homogenous, then refrigerate for 20 minutes. (Get started on WHITE CHOCOLATE MOUSSE while you wait.)

 03 Using an electric mixer, whisk together cream and sugar until somewhat firm spikes start forming. Using a spatula, delicately combine whipped cream with cooled chocolate preparation, then refrigerate for 2 hours.

WHITE CHOCOLATE MOUSSE

 04 Coarsely chop white chocolate and reserve. Using a knife, seed vanilla clove. Bring cream to a boil on medium heat, while stirring, and add in both the clove and seeds. Simmer for 1 minute, then remove from heat and discard the clove.

 05 Crack eggs and discard whites. Wash and reserve cracked shells for serving. Whisk yolks together with sugar until homogenous, then gradually incorporate warm vanilla cream. Put it all back in a pot and cook on low heat, stirring constantly, until mixture thickens (do not bring to a boil).

 06 Remove from heat and stir in chocolate. Let sit for 1 minute, then mix with a spoon until homogenous. Cover and refrigerate for 2 hours.

 07 Whisk cooled preparation with an electric mixer until somewhat firm spikes start forming, then reserve.

MATCHA-GREEN TEA FOAM*

 08 Bring water to a boil, remove from heat and infuse tea for 10 minutes. Mix in matcha powder. Let sit to cool, then transfer to a rectangular, flat-bottomed bowl.

 09 Sprinkle in SOY LECITHIN. Using a hand blender, blend for 3 to 4 minutes, then let sit for 5 minutes. To serve, collect foam using a spoon. If needed and to obtain more foam, repeat this step.

HIBISCUS-POMEGRANATE FOAM*

 10 Crush seeds in a bowl. Bring water to a boil, remove from heat, add in seeds and tea bags and infuse for 10 minutes. Let sit to cool, then transfer to a rectangular, flat-bottomed bowl. Repeat step 9.

GRAPEFRUIT FOAM*

 11 Pour juice into a rectangular, flat-bottomed bowl, then repeat step 9.

ASSEMBLY

 12 Using a pastry bag, divide chocolate mousses between egg shells and top with foams. The matcha-green tea and grapefruit go well with the white chocolate, while the pomegranate-hibiscus is a great fit for the dark chocolate.

TROPICAL
CAPSULE DUO

DIFFICULTY   3/5
ACTIVE TIME   0:30
TOTAL TIME   2:05
*TIPS ON SPHERES   P. 46

INGREDIENTS

POACHED APRICOTS WITH WINE

2 ¾ cup (670 ml) fresh apricots
1 cup (250 ml) water
¾ cup (190 ml) Sauvignon blanc
2 tbs (30 ml) honey

2 rosemary sprigs

BLACKBERRY JUICE SPHERES

3 cups (750 ml) blackberries
1 tbs (15 ml) honey
½ tsp (2.5 ml) CALCIUM LACTATE
1 sachet (2 g) SODIUM ALGINATE

PUMPKIN & SUNFLOWER BUTTER

1 cup (250 ml) shelled, unsalted sunflower seeds
½ cup (125 ml) shelled, unsalted pumpkin seeds
2 tbs (30 ml) flaxseed
¼ cup (65 ml) sunflower oil
1 tbs (15 ml) honey

TO SERVE

purple basil
extra rosemary

DIRECTIONS

POACHED APRICOTS WITH WINE

 01 Halve apricots and pit them. In a pot, bring water, wine and honey to a boil, then remove from heat. Add in apricots and rosemary and let sit, at room temperature, for 2 hours (start making BLACKBERRY JUICE SPHERES 30 minutes in), then refrigerate apricots (discard everything else). Serve cool.

BLACKBERRY JUICE **SPHERES***

 02 Using a juicer, extract juice from blackberries. Filter 3/4 of a cup of the juice. In a blender, combine with honey and CALCIUM LACTATE until completely dissolved. Pour mixture into small, demi-spherical molds and let sit in the freezer for 1 hour or until the spheres are frozen (While you wait, make PUMPKIN & SUNFLOWER SEED BUTTER.)

 03 In a rectangular, flat-bottomed bowl and using a hand blender, dissolve SODIUM ALGINATE in water. Let sit for 15 minutes.

 04 Unmold frozen spheres in alginate bath. Let sit for 3 minutes while gently stirring once in a while to prevent the spheres from touching.

 05 Fill a medium-sized bowl with water. Using a slotted spoon, delicately collect the spheres and briefly rinse them in the water, then remove excess water from each sphere by applying a piece of paper towel on the bottom of the spoon. Reserve.

PUMPKIN & SUNFLOWER BUTTER

 06 In a large pan, toast sunflower and pumpkin seeds on medium heat, stirring often, for 2 minutes. Remove from heat and let cool.

 07 In a food processor, pulse seeds into a fine grind. Then, continue blending while gradually pouring oil in, until homogenous and smooth (use a rubber spatula to scrape mixture off the food processor's inner walls). Finally, blend in honey and transfer to a jar. The butter will keep for up to 1 week at room temperature.

ASSEMBLY

 08 Start with some pumpkin and sunflower seed butter on the bottom of each plate, then top with a poached apricot and a blackberry sphere. Respectively garnish with rosemary and purple basil.

JASMINE
BALLOONS

DIFFICULTY 3/5
ACTIVE TIME 0:20
TOTAL TIME 1:20
*TIPS ON SPHERES P. 46

INGREDIENTS

JASMINE TEA SPHERES

1 cup (250 ml) water
2 jasmine tea bags
1 tsp (5 ml) honey
small edible flowers
½ tsp (2.5 ml) CALCIUM LACTATE
1 sachet (2 g) SODIUM ALGINATE

TO SERVE

a pot of your favorite green tea
(jasmine or other)

DIRECTIONS

JASMINE TEA **SPHERES***

01 Bring water to a boil and remove from heat. Place tea bags in hot water and let sit for 5 minutes. While you wait for the tea to steep, place flowers in small, demi-spherical molds (1 to 2 flowers per demi-sphere)

02 In a bowl and using a spoon, combine jasmine tea, honey and CALCIUM LACTATE until the calcium lactate has dissolved. Pour mixture into prepared demi-spherical molds and let sit in the freezer for 1 hour or until the spheres are frozen.

03 In a rectangular, flat-bottomed bowl and using a hand blender, dissolve SODIUM ALGINATE in water. Let sit for 15 minutes.

04 Unmold frozen tea spheres in alginate bath. Let sit for 3 minutes while gently stirring once in a while to prevent the spheres from touching.

05 Fill a medium-sized bowl with water. Using a slotted spoon, delicately collect the spheres and briefly rinse them in the water, then remove excess water from each sphere by applying a piece of paper towel on the bottom of the spoon. Reserve.

ASSEMBLY

06 Fill clear glasses with tea, place 2 to 3 jasmine tea spheres in each glass, and serve.

CAPPUCCINO NOUVEAU GENRE

INGREDIENTS

COFFEE

freshly brewed coffee, hot
sweetened condensed milk, to taste
ice cubes

CHILI-TONKA FOAM

1 cup (250 ml) soymilk
2 tsp (10 ml) chili powder
6 tonka beans, grated
1 sachet (2 g) SOY LECITHIN

NOTE

You can replace the sweetened condensed
milk with your favorite plant-based milk.

DIRECTIONS

COFFEE

 01 In a pitcher and using a spoon, dissolve condensed milk in hot coffee. Refrigerate until cold, or place in the freezer for about an hour to save time.

CHILI & TONKA **FOAM***

 02 In a rectangular, flat-bottomed bowl, combine soymilk, chili powder and grated beans with a spoon. Then, using a hand blender, dissolve SOY LECITHIN into the solution. Mix for 3 to 4 minutes, then let sit for 5 minutes.

ASSEMBLY

 03 Pour cold coffee in clear glasses and top with chili-tonka foam.

NEW
OLD FASHIONED

DIFFICULTY   3/5
ACTIVE TIME   0:15
TOTAL TIME   1:15
*TIPS ON SPHERES   P. 46

INGREDIENTS

SIMPLE SYRUP

2 parts sugar
1 part water

COGNAC SPHERES

1 fl oz (30 ml) simple syrup
2 fl oz (60 ml) cognac
2 fl oz (60 ml) club soda
2 cups (500 ml) water
¼ tsp (1.25 ml) CALCIUM LACTATE
1 sachet (2 g) SODIUM ALGINATE

TO SERVE

2 fl oz (60 ml) bourbon
4 dashes Angostura bitters

TO GARNISH

lemon peel spirals
maraschino cherries

DIRECTIONS

SIMPLE SYRUP

01 In a pot, bring water to a boil. Pour sugar in and continue boiling, while stirring constantly, until the sugar has completely dissolved and the mixture has thickened just a bit.

02 Remove from heat and let cool down completely, then bottle! You can make as little or as much syrup as you think you'll require over the next few days.

COGNAC **SPHERES***

03 In a bowl and using a spoon, combine simple syrup, cognac, club soda and CALCIUM LACTATE until the calcium lactate has dissolved, then filter mixture using a sieve. Pour the filtered mixture into small, demi-spherical molds and let sit in the freezer for 1 hour or until the spheres are frozen.

04 In a rectangular, flat-bottomed bowl and using a hand blender, dissolve SODIUM ALGINATE in water. Let sit for 15 minutes.

05 Unmold frozen cognac spheres in alginate bath. Let sit for 3 minutes while gently stirring once in a while to prevent the spheres from touching.

06 Fill a medium-sized bowl with water. Using a slotted spoon, delicately collect the spheres and briefly rinse them in the water, then remove excess water from each sphere by applying a piece of paper towel on the bottom of the spoon. Reserve.

ASSEMBLY

07 Place a few cognac spheres in a glass. In a cocktail shaker, shake together bourbon and bitters, then pour into the glass and garnish with lemon peel spiral and maraschino cherry.

IF YOU'VE NEVER HEARD OF CANADIAN FOOD PHOTOGRAPHER SYLVIE RACICOT, [THIS] SUMPTUOUS MOLECULAR FOOD PORN [...] WILL SOON MAKE HER A HOUSEHOLD NAME.

— **FINE DINING LOVERS**
THE ONLINE MAGAZINE OF
S. PELLEGRINO & ACQUA PANNA

Molécule-R
photography by
Sylvie Racicot
chezvalois.com

MOLECULAR STYLING DELUXE KIT

Available on MOLECULE-R.com

DROP AND INJECT

DIVIDE AND MAKE INCISIONS

GARNISH AND EMBELLISH

HOLD AND SPREAD

TRIM AND CUT

REMOVE AND REPLACE